THE ABCs OF RETIREMENT

How to Not Work and Love It

THE ABCs OF RETIREMENT

How to Not Work and Love It

TERRY CHAMBERLAIN

thistledown press

Second printing, 2003, Third printing 2014

Thistledown Press Ltd.
410 2nd Avenue North
Saskatoon, Saskatchewan
S7K 2C3

Canadian Cataloguing in Publication Data
Chamberlain, Terry, 1938–
The ABCs of retirement
ISBN 978-1-894345-49-1
I. Retirement—Humor. 2. Canadian wit and humor (English)*
I. Title.
PN6231.R44C42 2002 C818'.5402 C2002-910957-4

Cover photograph by Brian Kuhlmann/Masterfile
Cover and book design by Jackie Forrie
Printed and bound in Canada

Thistledown Press gratefully acknowledges the financial assistance of the Canada Council for the Arts, the Saskatchewan Arts Board, and the Government of Canada through the Canada Book Fund for its publishing program.

To the long-retired, the just-retired, and soon to be retired: enjoy

FOREWORD

I have spent my adult life so far in four occupations: I have been a Teacher, a Farmer, a Writer and a Retired Person. Generally I have been more successful at the last role than at any of the others. I seem to have a natural aptitude for doing nothing.

In 1999 my book *The ABCs of Farming* went on the market. It was well received by the public and consequently my publisher suggested a follow-up "ABCs" volume. After considering some options — Teaching, Parenting, Grandparenting and Medicare among them — I settled on Retirement.

It seemed a natural, me being so good at it and all. As well, Retirement is not just about Doing Nothing, you see. Although you may want to Do Nothing, may indeed seem to be Doing Nothing in retirement, there is one thing you cannot avoid doing, and that is Aging. And since I have aged — without any effort on my part — fairly well so far, I felt I might have some wisdom to share on that subject as well. It is, after all, a topic that can take in many others: Grandchildren, Medicine, Menopause, Brain Cell Deterioration and Leisure Activities for Seniors, for example.

Though the book is obviously — at least I hope it is obvious — intended to be humorous rather than serious, a few themes emerged as it took shape.

One is my contempt for the currently fashionable cult of the workaholic. It's not that I don't like work. Indeed I do like it, but not very much. Not, at any rate, to the extent of overdoing it in order to impress others. I have a few pet projects that require some effort — these unfocused scribblings among them — but am careful to set aside enough large blocks of unscheduled time to have the freedom to do whatever I want on a moment's notice. Otherwisc why retire? You might as well hang on to your full-time job and continue to get paid for it.

Another theme you will notice is my criticism of the Baby Boomers. Now I am not prejudiced against any Baby Boomers as individuals. Some of my best friends are Boomers. Not only would I not mind if my brother were to marry one, in fact one of my brothers did, and so, for that matter, did I.

It's just that, well, the Boomers had things so good when they were growing up, and they had so much freedom as young adults, and they so dominated the country by sheer numbers that they were able to have everything their way, and — well, are you beginning to think I'm envious? Well, let's be honest here. Sure I'm envious. I admit it.

But surely it's a duty (as well as a legitimate privilege) of my generation to resent the Boomers and to point out their faults. For their improvement, of course. And since they have for decades thrived on, relished even, the envy, resentment and disapproval of their elders, I am in fact doing them a favour.

It is in this spirit that, as the leading edge of the Baby Boomer generation begins to retire, I offer them, as well as older retirees, this little volume of easy-to-swallow advice and information that I learned by trial and error after I took my own fateful leap into the perilous world of post-employment.

But don't look too hard for themes here. One of the mistakes most of us made during our working lives was taking ourselves too seriously. Let's not perpetuate it in retirement.

ABSURD.

The fact you are actually old enough to retire. Why, only yesterday you were just in your prime, at the top of your form, and you still are, right? Well, no. (See **AGING.**)

ACHIEVEMENT.

Some people are reluctant to retire until they've "made their mark"; achieved something that will bring them some measure of recognition and/or wealth. My advice: with your level of talent and competence it's not going to happen, is it? Quit while you're ahead.

ADDICTION.

In your mad scramble to succeed in the world of work you quite likely gave up many of your favourite vices. Now you will have the time and resources to pick up on them again. Isn't that exciting?

Well, maybe not. Many who thought that way have discovered that they now get too tired to stay out late, their stomachs can't handle the booze any more, and the objects of their carnal desires can outrun them. Ah, well, who said life was fair? (See also **ALCOHOL, FANTASY, MODERATION, NARCOTICS.**)

ADVICE.

It is a privilege to receive advice from the wise (see **RETIREMENT ADVICE**). But it is a far sweeter privilege, as we age, to *provide* advice to those who have not been blessed with our wisdom. Either way, this is a commodity for which the supply consistently outstrips the demand. (See also **CORRECTIVE CRITICISM, MORALITY, PREACHING, WISDOM.**)

AGING.

If you are contemplating retirement, you're aging. Like it or not (and who does?) it happens. If you are one of the Baby Boomer generation you are particularly p'd off and astonished, because you always criticized Old Fogeys and never expected to be one — though your definition of "old" keeps receding, like the horizon, as you approach it.

The ill effects of aging are obvious and are covered in other parts of this book. However there are a number of advantages to growing old. Consider:

1. Once you are classified as an Old Fogey you no longer have to keep up with the latest in clothing styles. This is a relief, especially in the present era of the Loose and Sloppy look, with duds so ill-fitting you can turn around in them without moving the fabric. And those oversize shorts in garish floral patterns: any man of my (pre-Boomer) generation, given a choice between the firing squad or wearing a pair of those for a day would instantly reply, "Hand me the blindfold and tell the guys to shoot straight." My discount store jeans and ball caps are just fine now, thank you. (Many female

retirees and some males — I hope I'm not being chauvinistic here — will not, I suspect, share my ultra-casual attitude in this matter.)

2. When responsibilities are divided up within a group, you are no longer assigned the hardest tasks. Maybe you didn't get them when you were young either, but now you don't have to wonder if it's because you're considered incompetent.
3. When you are in a planning group and some young firebrand comes up with an inspired, brand new scheme that he promotes with great excitement, you can sit back, smile knowingly, say, "Sorry, it won't work. We tried that in the 60s," and watch the glow fade from his face. It gives you a kind of perverse satisfaction.
4. If you wish to refuse an unwelcome request for your time or labour you can simply beg off by pleading fatigue or arthritis. Everyone will believe you.
5. No one expects you to remember anything. This last point is a vital one for me. Since childhood I have been cursed with a faulty memory, and it was often embarrassing. When teaching I would think of something I needed, get up from my classroom desk, stride purposefully down the hallway to the front office, throw open the door, stop suddenly and stare blankly at the secretary. She would wonder what the hell I was doing there. So would I. Actually it's not so much that my memory is poor, but that it's selective in a rather weird way. For example, I once drove without valid licence plates for six months because I forgot to

pay the second installment on the fee, but I remember that Jay Silverheels played Tonto on the Lone Ranger series back in the sixties, and I know Kathmandu is the capital of Nepal. I can remember just about anything, you see, as long as it's totally useless. But who expects anything else from you once you're over the hill? (See also **DIET, FACELIFT, HAIR, HILL, LIBIDO, MENOPAUSE, MENTAL AGILITY, MEMORY, PLASTIC SURGERY, SEX, SIGNS OF AGING, TUMMY TUCK, WEIGHT, WISDOM.**)

ALCOHOL.

A friend of mine told me he came to realize one day that his drinking and his work were beginning to interfere with one another, so he quit. Working, that is. Now most of us do not look forward to retirement as an opportunity to become full-time drunks. However getting into the sauce too often is sometimes a temptation to retired people who find too much time on their hands and not enough challenges in their lives. If that happens to you, take a tip from me: If ever I find I have too much leisure time on my hands — and that hasn't happened yet, by the way — I'll simply let my wife know that, and she'll immediately find enough for me to do to take care of my spare time for the next several weeks. (Female readers will please forgive me for approaching this subject from a male point of view, but I don't know any men who are constantly looking for chores for their wives to do. And that, of course, is because women have always — a holdover from the stay-at-home mom days — found enough to do around the place to keep themselves busy.)

Male or female, what you need is an activity or hobby that will help fill your time and meet your need for challenge — anything from restoring antique mousetraps to collecting toenail clippings. And if you need any further incentive remember: Hangovers really do hurt more than they used to. (See also **ADDICTION, GOAL, HOBBY, MODERATION, NARCOTICS.**)

ANACHRONISM.

This concept is best defined by an example, and I will use one from my own experience. When the conversation comes around to music and song, and I mention that a certain singer reminds me of Buddy Knox, and everyone looks at me inquiringly, and someone says, "Who's Buddy Knox?" I know I'm an anachronism. (See also **HILL, MUSEUM, NOSTALGIA, PAST.**)

ANTIQUE. SEE MUSEUM, NOSTALGIA.

ARTHRITIS. SEE BONES.

ARTS AND CRAFTS.

I have always envied those who, in their spare time or upon retirement, take up woodcarving, painting, cabinet making, leatherwork, pottery, or restoring antique furniture, clocks, automobiles and the like. They become absorbed in these pursuits and find them very rewarding. I would try some of them myself were it not for a couple of impediments: no talent and no patience. My wife, who is much craftier than

I, takes great pleasure in converting almost anything — wood, plastic, paper, glass, tin cans, bottles, egg cartons — into objects (flower pots, Christmas decorations and the like) of usefulness and beauty. So adept is she at recycling these materials that we have to borrow garbage from the neighbours to put out in our back alley trash can.

AUTOBIOGRAPHY. See **MEMOIRS, REMINISCENCE.**

AUTOMOBILE.

The part played by the motorized vehicle in the lives of North Americans is impossible to exaggerate. 99.7% of us have been a passenger in one, 88.3% of us as adults have driven one, 75.8% of us have eaten restaurant meals in one, 63.4% of us use one in our jobs, 35.2% of us were conceived in one and 10.5% of us will die in one. (The figures are mine, based on lifelong observation, which is correct, within a 47% margin of error, seven times out of 20.) The vehicle's importance increases, if anything, after retirement, when we have more time to travel. If you are over 60 you will have noticed, as I have, the following reaction: a news story mentions the incidence of traffic accidents among older drivers and suggests it may be necessary to re-test them every three years or so. A brief wave of icy fear sweeps over your body. (See also **SADISM**, example # 3, **TRAVEL.**)

B

BABY BOOMER.

Person born between 1946 and 1960. The Baby Boomers are the most numerous and influential generation in North America. I was born eight years too early to be one of them. I hate them. Ever since the 1960s they have been catered to by governments, the media, the entertainment industry and business in general. My generation, sandwiched between the Boomers and their parents, was too young to get in on the glory of being War and Depression survivors and too old to get in on Free Love and Doing Your Own Thing. Talk about an awkward age. My contemporaries and I have consequently condemned the Boomers mercilessly for their presumptuous, arrogant, self-indulgent behaviour, and we would have given anything to have gotten in on it.

However, since the older Boomers are beginning to retire and many of the younger ones are thinking about it, much of this book's contents is addressed to them. Some of my references to them are uncomplimentary. Some are downright bitter. But they'll have to put up with it, because I have compiled for them priceless information (for a small price) on making the inevitable transition from labour to leisure.

I should add, in the interests of fairness, cowardice, and an unwillingness to alienate a huge chunk of my targeted market, that I have many good friends and dear relatives (not to mention a wife) among the Boomers. As individuals I relate quite well to them. It is only as a group that they become insufferable.

BABYSITTING.

Babysitting for grandchildren is the second commonest (after the afternoon nap) pastime of retirees whose children live nearby. As a rule this is a pleasant experience, though now and then it can be tiring. You soon notice that, just as stairs are made steeper and newspaper print smaller than when you were young, infants are also heavier, children more energetic and their voices louder (which is strange, because you are deafer). You now realize, with some guilt, that you unloaded your own children on their grandparents a little oftener and longer than you should have. Indeed there is nothing sweeter than having the grandchildren come to stay with you, though having them go home again is a close second. (See also **CHILDREN, GRANDCHILDREN.**)

BED.

A piece of furniture, the significance of which changes as you age. At one time you heard the phrase "going to bed" and thought, Wow! Adventure! Excitement! Passion! Now, more often, you think, Ah, Peace, Quiet, Immobility, Sleep. And you suspect that when your spouse tells someone you are "good in bed" (s)he means you don't snore much or steal the blankets. (See **LIBIDO, SEX, SIGNS OF AGING # 8.**)

BIRD WATCHING.

This hobby is rapidly gaining in popularity as the population ages. What you do, I'm told, is go out where birds hang around, watch them through binoculars and then record your observations in a notebook. I decided to try this, went to a nearby wooded area with my field glasses and spent about an hour watching several birds. And here, according to my notebook, is what birds do. (a)Fly around. (b)Eat bugs. (c)Sit around on branches a lot. (d)Scrap a lot — using considerable profanity — with other birds that want to sit on the same branch. (There was no shortage of branches, so birds, we must conclude, are either very belligerent or mentally challenged.) (e)Sing some (not bad on melody, a bit lacking in lyrics and beat). (f)Poop a lot. An awful lot, actually. OK, I'm just being a smart-ass of course. I know many people who find bird watching to be a challenging and fascinating activity. We have a bird feeder in our yard during the winter and get dozens of the colourful little freeloaders every day — a pleasure to behold.

BONES.

Your skeleton is an indispensable part of you. Without its support you would be nothing but a shapeless pile of flesh, unable to move except by rolling along the ground like a very large and repulsive worm. In the days of your carefree youth you no doubt took your bones for granted and were generally unaware of their presence unless you broke one. With age, however, almost every bone in your body will eventually find a way of letting you know it's there. (See also **SIGNS OF AGING.**)

BOOKS.

More time for reading is one of the major blessings of retirement. Read more. Watch less TV. Buy lots of books. Encourage your friends to buy lots of books. Suggest this one.

BOREDOM.

What? You worked your butt off all your life, yearning for freedom, now your time is free, and you're bored? God help you, but if He can't, perhaps I can: See FAQ, questions 3 and 4, also **GOALS, LEISURE, RETIREMENT ADVICE.**

BOSS.

Many are the employees who, approaching retirement, dream of that last day of work when they can, just before leaving for the last time, perform one or more of the following services for the Boss: (a) thumb their noses at her, (b) give him the one-finger salute, (c) moon him, (d) punch him in the nose, (e) shake her hand, tell her what a pleasure it's been to work for her, then collapse into a fit of hysterical laughter. What they *should* do, however, is fall upon their knees and offer him or her sincerest gratitude. Why? Because many times over the coming years they'll think of the Boss and remind themselves once again what a blessed thing retirement is.

BRAIN CELL DETERIORATION.

You have no doubt heard that as people grow older their brain cells — which are irreplaceable — begin to die off. Now I was never terribly concerned about this. After all, the brain has multi-billions of cells, and if you lose a few thousand now and then, well, that's like hauling a few buckets of water out of a lake (though some of us have a larger lake than others). However, my neighbour's four-year-old daughter recently asked me several questions (among them: Why did God make mosquitoes and broccoli? If the sky wasn't blue what colour would it be? Where do Zamboni drivers go in the summer?) that I could come up with no answers for whatever. That got me worried. Am I losing it? Oh well, if ignorance is bliss I may soon be the happiest guy in the home. (See also **MENTAL AGILITY, MEMORY.**)

BRIDGE.

Bridge building is one of the costliest and most demanding of construction projects. Many of us don't appreciate this — I speak here from personal experience — until the later decades of our lives. (See **DENTIST, DENTURES.**)

CAMPING.

A favourite activity of many retirees, one they have long looked forward to having more time for. Who could fail to appreciate the down-to-earth experiences of camping

Like sucking in deep lungfulls of fresh, pine-scented air, and then coughing up the mosquitoes you swallowed in the process. Hearing the plaintive night cry of the loon, along with those of the party crowd across the campground, a booming stereo providing accompaniment. Listening to the patter of summer rain on the camper roof at night, and arguing over who should go out to see if the camera got left on the picnic table. Reflecting on the fact that the best things in life really are free — aside, of course, from the $25 per night camp fee, the $45 park access charge, the cost of your camper and the gasoline used to pull it. Enjoying an intimacy with wildlife — like the time our dog, sleeping inside with us, charged at the door and knocked it open, allowing the skunk which had excited her to discharge his full load directly into the camper. Talk about getting intimate with nature. (See also **NATURE.**)

CARDS.

Playing cards — particularly Bridge, Whist and Cribbage — is a favourite pastime of older folk, though all ages enjoy it. By retirement age most of us have learned — as I did one night forty years ago — that wagering big cash on the whims of the little pasteboards is for the Fool and the Sucker (I held both titles then). By now we know that winning the right to smirk triumphantly at the player whose ace you have just trumped is worth more than gold.

CHILDREN:

A source of comfort to the aging retiree? Well, up to a point. There are four distinct stages, you see, in the relationship between parents and their children:

Stage 1: When your children are small they regard you as a god, a heroic figure who can take care of anything.

Stage 2: For a few years beginning in their early teens they see you as a festering embarrassment, so uncool and uncouth that they will go to any lengths to avoid being seen with you in public.

Stage 3: By their mid-twenties they begin to want to have you around again and seem amused rather than embarrassed by your outdated tastes, political and social attitudes. Your grandchildren begin to act as bonds between the generations; their parents' enthusiasm to share their children's lives with you indicates that they don't believe your quaint habits and beliefs will have a totally harmful influence after all. Or maybe they just want a free babysitter now and then. Of course when your grandchildren are very young there's a good chance you can regain some of the hero worship you experienced in Stage 1.

Stage 4: By the time you retire, your world view and your children's — they having gone through many of the same rough spots and faced some of the same harsh realities of life that you have — have moved closer together, and you are fully enjoying one another's company. Except now and then you catch them looking at you — perhaps after telling them a joke you told a few hours earlier — in such a way that you suspect they are wondering how soon they'll have to put you away and where. (See also **BABYSITTING, GRANDCHILDREN.**)

CHOLESTEROL.

A substance found in food which makes it so tasty it cannot possibly be good for you, so cut it out right now. No doubt your doctor has already told you to cut down on the cholesterol in your diet. This is relatively easy to arrange. Simply make a list of all the foods you enjoy, make another list of the foods you don't much care for, cross off everything on the first list and learn to subsist on the rest. In fact, however, there are good (HDL) and bad (LDL) forms of cholesterol, and the good one (which shows up under a microscope as tiny blobs, each wearing a white hat) can apparently help chase the bad one (microscopic blobs with black hats) out of the system. For a list of HDL foods check with a health professional; some of them are actually edible (the HDL foods, that is, not the health professionals). (See also **FOOD, NUTRITION, WEIGHT.**)

CHORES.

No doubt there are many chores and projects about the house and yard that you have neglected while working but expect to complete in short order once you retire. Sorry. I hate to disappoint you, but it doesn't work that way. Mind you, maybe it's just me; I admit to being somewhat energy-challenged (my wife uses a different word here, a four-letter one at that). As a matter of fact, I believe there is a certain gender difference at play here — see **GENDER DIFFERENCES, #6**. As I said to my wife one day recently, I really would like to finish cutting the grass and nailing up those loose boards on the fence, but that would be foolish. It was a hot day, you see, and what with that leaky ozone layer, all those ultraviolet rays and such — well, you can't say we haven't been warned about the consequences. After all, if I don't look out for my health who will? Her response indicates that she has a rather casual attitude about my well-being. She says I have used the same excuse every day this week for not getting any chores done, and that I didn't do them last week because it was too damp and cold. Well it was. (See also **DOMESTIC HARMONY, HOME IMPROVEMENT, HOUSEWORK.**)

CLOTHING.

You will still need some in retirement, unless you plan to move to a nudist colony in some southern land, but now you can wear what you want (chuck the tie, burn the pantyhose) instead of what you're expected to. (See **AGING, advantage #1**; also **COOL, FASHION, TRENDS.**)

CODGER. See **COOT, FOGEY.**

COLLECTING.

Many retirees are scroungers, and they will collect almost anything, including coins, bottle tops, fishing lures, guns, spoons, plates, salt shakers, clocks, vinyl records, books, classic cars and antique tractors. One Alberta couple collects barns. (Check out your storage and display space before you try that one.) My wife collects pig paraphernalia. She has literally hundreds of porcine items: salt and pepper shakers, pictures, plaques, cups, fridge magnets, T-shirts, you name it. Which is fine, but whenever a visitor to our house tells another, "Esther collects pigs, you know," and they turn and look at me, I somehow resent it.

COMPETITIVENESS.

If you are human you are competitive. Even if you swear you're not. Even if you're a dedicated socialist. And you will not lose this quality with age. A conversation with the sweetest and gentlest of little old ladies will soon reveal that she considers herself to be just a bit sweeter and gentler than certain other little old ladies of her acquaintance. (See also **LEISURE, SPORTS.**)

COMPUTER.

My brother once told me his wife and kids keep buying him digital watches, not the cheap, discount store versions, but good ones. He makes use of them for a while — some have very admirable functions — and then of course he has to throw them away. Why? Well, because he's over 60, and no one anywhere near that age can set the time on a digital watch when that procedure becomes necessary. Neither can they program a VCR or get beyond the rudiments of using a computer. It wasn't until well after the middle of the 20th century, you see, that hospitals began putting drops of a secret chemical into the formula of newborns, one which confers an Electronic Literacy Capability on anyone born after that date. The rest of us are hopeless, except for a few individuals here and there who are not really normal.

I use a computer for some functions now, but only after being hounded into it by my wife. (She's only a few years younger than I, but seems to be on the other side of the Digital Stupidity Gap.) My use of the thing is pretty limited though, and when I'm on it I like my wife to be within screaming-for-help distance.

Many seniors are now discovering the benefits and pleasures of the PC and the Internet. Therefore I would advise you, upon retirement if not sooner, to call in an electronic communications consultant — your seven-year-old grandchild will do nicely — and learn how properly to operate the beast. (See also **OBSOLETE, TECHNOLOGICAL CONFUSION.**)

CONDOMINIUM. See **DWELLING.**

CONTACT LENS. See **SPECTACLES.**

CONVERSATION.

Ever since the days of old codgers sitting on benches in front of the general store, the gabfest has been a favourite pastime of retirees, one that requires little monetary expense, physical effort, or (in most cases) mental exertion.

You will notice that the topics of conversation favoured by you and your cronies has changed over the years and will continue to change, from (1) Gossip, School, Girls/Boys, Sex, Parties, Clothing and Sports (active), to (2) Gossip, Jobs, Children, Houses, Cars, Politics and Sports (spectator), to (3) Gossip, Grandchildren, Travel, Reminiscences, Surgery and Medication.

Gossip, of course, is a cherished topic at all ages and for both sexes. It's not necessarily a bad thing. After all, you would not endlessly discuss the affairs (I use the word in its widest sense here) of your friends and relatives if you were not interested in those people and did not have some concern for their well-being. Sometimes it's just an indication that you are there, ready to help, when you hear of someone in trouble. (And if you think that last point is the chief reason for gossip, I have some ocean-front real estate in central Saskatchewan I can give you a good deal on.)

There's another good thing about gossip. Back in the Stone Age, you see, if someone offended you, you would get even by caving his skull in with your club or running her through with your spear. This was not — considering the human tendency to take offense — conducive to maintaining the tribal population at a large enough level for a viable defense against other tribes. With the invention of gossip it became possible to destroy the offender's reputation instead of his/her life. This was a much more civilized response, and had the added benefit of the culprit remaining alive to suffer the pain of your verbal backstabbing.

The notion that women are more given to idle chatter than men is, of course, unfounded. I know men who can chin-wag with the best of them. And I know there are women who are not big talkers; indeed they can be found right here in my hometown. In fact I know both of them. (See also **REMINISCENCE.**)

COOL.

This adjective was just coming into fashion when I was a teen and became a term of religious anointing during the '60s. Then it referred more to attitude (arrogant), morality (anything goes), clothing (scruffy), hair (scruffier), language (irreverent), folk and rock bands (uglier the better). Retirement-age Boomers still use the word, but it has lost most of its in-your-face air and has come to mean something more like, well — *nice*. As in "Your new necktie is pretty cool." It's enough to make Hendrix and Lennon turn over in their graves. (See also **FASHION, TRENDS.**)

COOT.

Noun — always preceded by the adjective "old" — denoting "senior gentleman". ("No, Dad, the lady didn't say you're 'so cute', she said . . . ") See also **FOGEY.**

CORRECTIVE CRITICISM.

Perhaps you have recently begun to notice that the upcoming generations tend to be weak, irresponsible, demanding, idle, dependent, self-indulgent, morally deficient and insufficiently grateful for the many blessings bestowed upon them by your generation. And it's your job to let them know about it. How else will they learn? Try not to enjoy it so much that it shows, however. (See also **ADVICE, LECTURE, MORALITY, PREACHING, WISDOM.**)

CRONE. See **HAG.**

CROSSWORD PUZZLES.

It's amazing how many people are addicted to these little teasers.

They're an ideal pastime for the over-the-hill swinger: cheaper than concerts, less exhausting than dancing, less debilitating than booze, and you can enjoy them in bed with no guilt feelings afterwards.

CURLING.

A game very popular with Canadian seniors as it is not overly active or violent and does not move along at a breathtaking pace. Those are the same qualities, however, that cause some sports fans to condemn it as boring. To which I respond: have you watched any golf lately? It is extremely popular with both old and young, yet it makes curling look positively wild, crazy and hyperactive by comparison.

D

DEATH.

Don't want to hear about it? Well, you see, it's this way: If none of us really can escape such inevitables as death, taxes and singing toilet paper commercials, we may as well laugh at them. Besides, no one will ever, at any other time, say such flattering things about you as the guy who'll do your eulogy. (See also **EULOGY, OBITUARY, UNDERTAKER, WILL.**)

DENTIST.

As a person of retirement age, you can always be sure that even if friends grow tired of you, your family neglects you, your spouse leaves you and your dog turns his back on you, your dentist will still love you. You are not just his bread and butter, you see, but his Lexus, his summer cottage and his kids' college education as well. He has a host of associates — clinical assistants, dental lab technicians, oral surgeons and the like — who frequently consult with one another professionally to determine how much you are likely to have in your bank account.

Case in point: I had some extensive reconstruction and installation of hardware done in my mouth about three years ago, the cost of which was a bit more than the only new vehicle I ever bought, about fifteen times what my first car cost, and around one third of what I paid for my first house, a fairly new one. My dentist and his staff beam with joy whenever I walk into the clinic.

Being a dentist at the time the appearance-obsessed Baby Boomers and their mouths are aging must be truly blissful — like a licence to print money. (See **BRIDGE, DENTURES.**)

DENTURES.

My parents — both of whom had a set — called them "false teeth", and most of their contemporaries seemed to have artificial choppers by the time they reached middle age. My personal experience with dentures is limited to a series of "partial" upper plates obtained to replace two front teeth I lost to hockey and other youthful indiscretions. None of them lasted a year without breaking and requiring repair; some of them fit too loosely, and one "el cheapo" version I got a special deal on made me look a bit like Northern Dancer. After about 35 years of putting up with these contraptions I finally had the last one replaced with some extensive bridgework about three years ago, after undergoing oral surgery to prepare for it. This solution seems so far to have eliminated all the problems, except how to repair my severely damaged bank account.

Dentures are often a source of fascination for small children. The young son of an acquaintance once said of his grandmother, to a friend, "She's the kind the teeth come out of." (See also **BRIDGE, DENTIST.**)

DIET.

Centuries-old paintings and sculptures tell us fashion once dictated that females be properly padded with enough fatty tissue that hugging one of them would give a feeling of substance and comfort. Today's fashion dictates that it will be more like embracing a coat rack. As for men, in past generations a generous waistline in middle age was the mark of a solid, successful citizen, one who could afford leisure and good food. My parents, in fact, referred to a round belly on a man as a "corporation". But today it's called a "beer belly", a symbol of the much-derided "couch potato", while the successful man is expected to be lean and fit.

To conform to these ideals, the choice for the aging is clear: diet or exercise. For today's TV and junk food lovers this is like a choice between hell and purgatory. So it's not surprising that they turn with relief to commercial diet plans that promise to let you have your cake, eat it too and still get thin. (Further details under **FOOD** and **NUTRITION.** See also **EXERCISE, WEIGHT.**)

DIGNITY.

Many aging people, having lost their hair, teeth, short-term memory and agility, are determined not to lose their dignity; in fact they aim to enhance it. Some of them try to do this by refusing to smile much, by offering caustic criticism of just about everything that's happened since 1965, and by walking, chin up, with such a very deliberate air they are in danger of tripping and falling flat on their faces. Which we all long to see them do, figuratively or literally. (See also **GRAVITY, PRIDE.**)

DISGRUNTLEMENT.

I have often heard the complaint that old people become crabby and disgruntled. This is an unfair generalization; the few oldsters who are disgruntled now never were gruntled in the first place.

DISTINGUISHED.

Like many words young people use to describe the appearance of older folk, this adjective is intended as a compliment. But it doesn't make you feel complimented. It makes you feel old. How about — if you're male — "handsome", "cute", "sexy"? Much better, no? However, if you are female you will probably be described as "lovely", "beautiful" or — go figure — "handsome". (See also **MATRONLY, VENERABLE, WORD CHOICE.**)

DOCTOR. See **PHYSICIAN**.

DOMESTIC HARMONY.

During their working years many couples believe they are getting along just fine, often because they seldom see each other. Once they are thrown together 24 hours a day, however, they begin to discover things about each other — things that horrify them. So, assuming you want to stay together (after all, who else would have you now?), what can you do to smooth things over? The advice I am about to impart is totally from a male perspective — I can't help that. If you wish to get the view from the female side, ask any woman of your acquaintance and she'll be glad — eager, in fact — to tell you.

Here then are my suggestions for establishing a harmonious relationship with your wife:

1. Learn to communicate. This doesn't mean you have to agree with, understand, or even actually hear her criticisms of you (sometimes your mind is employed elsewhere, planning how to improve your golf stroke, for example). It simply means you must *show* a respectful attention. Nodding your head, glancing up now and then, and inserting an appropriate remark ("You have a point there", "Indeed", "Yes, I see", or the ever-popular "Yes, Dear") every two or three minutes will suit her just fine, since you seem to be listening but not interrupting.
2. Learn to read minds. You can't always depend on the spoken word. If you ask your wife what she wants for her birthday and she says "Nothing", do you assume you need not get her anything? If you tell her you're meeting your friends for poker Friday night and she says, "Go right ahead, enjoy yourself, I'll be just fine here at home by myself", do you really think she doesn't mind? Boy, do you have a lot to learn.
3. Show an interest in your wife's pastimes and projects. But don't overdo it. Many a retired man, finding too much time on his hands, intrudes himself daily into his wife's hobbies, work and other activities, offering

countless suggestions for improvement, to the point where she isn't sure whether she should shove him off the balcony or jump off herself. Better to stick to sharing pursuits that don't require much input on your part, e.g. listening to music, watching TV, sleeping. One other solution to sharing common problems is for each of you to participate in a different aspect of the same venture. For example my wife loves cooking and I love eating.

4. Learn to appreciate the difference between male and female humour. A friend of mine was once asked by his wife if he thought she was getting a bit overweight. "Not at all," he replied, but then could not resist adding, "not for a small pony." He has learned his lesson, of course, and is healing nicely. (See also **CHORES, GENDER DIFFERENCES, HOME IMPROVEMENT, HOUSEWORK, MARRIAGE, MENOPAUSE.**)

DWELLING.

Where to live is an important consideration upon retirement. If you live in a detached house, and if you enjoy fighting crabgrass and shoveling snow, you can continue to live there. If you want to chuck those chores and always be travel-ready, get a condominium. If you are the adventurous type and want to always be where would-be visiting relatives can't find you, get a motor home and keep it moving. If you are the weak, self-indulgent type who can no longer face the winters, you can flee down to a sunny southern retirement community, perhaps a gated one so you can keep the real world out. (I checked them out. Can't afford it. No, I'm not bitter.) If all these choices bewilder you and leave you stewing in indecision, worry not. Just hang on and eventually the options will, all on their own, narrow down to one. It's called a nursing home. (See also **HOME IMPROVEMENT, SNOWBIRDS, WINTER.**)

E

EASY CHAIR.

A blessing indeed for the retired and the aging, but it carries with it a hazard you should be aware of: see **SOFA.** (See also **FURNITURE, ROCKING CHAIR.**)

ENERGY.

One of the things that make some people want to keep working. If you steadfastly ignore it, however, it will eventually go away and quit bothering you. Some retirees make the mistake of carrying some of it with them into retirement, where it soon clutters up their days with a new range of activities. At this point you must decide to dismiss it from your life once and for all or be a slave to it until advanced age mercifully puts an end to it.

For an explanation of the physical and mental components of energy, ask someone else. I've sort of forgotten what it feels like, though I'm fairly sure I had some once. (See also **GOALS, WORK, WORKAHOLIC.**)

EULOGY.

Sooner or later you will be asked to give a eulogy for someone in your circle of friends and relatives. Occasionally you will find yourself hard-pressed for something positive to say, considering that it's not nice to tell fibs in church. It is possible, however, to comfort the guy's loved ones without actually lying. Examples:

"He truly was a family man." (He left a trail of family behind him in several cities.)

"He was a loyal friend." (Had to be; he owed all his friends money.)

"It was seldom you found Bob in anything but an upbeat, jolly mood." (Seldom found him sober either.)

"He had a great sense of humour." (Liked to dump crushed ice into people's pants.)

So why do you engage in such often undeserved flattery? Simple. Someone from the same crowd will do *your* eulogy one of these days, and you don't want to do anything to change the tradition of not getting too fussy about the truth. (See also **DEATH, OBITUARY, WILL.**)

EXERCISE.

There is nothing on this planet more admired in theory and hated in practice than exercise. Everyone knows how indispensable it is to the attainment of a sense of physical and mental well-being, to long-term health, to endurance and to an attractive appearance, and no generation has been so aware of its benefits as the Baby Boomers — particularly as they approach their senior years. Millions of them sign up for fitness programs in commercial gymnasiums and millions more buy home exercise devices — weights, treadmills, ab toners, butt shrinkers and the like. Up to that point it's a triumph of theory.

Then comes reality. For most of us, doing repetitive exercises is about as much fun as counting toothpicks. It may also be painful, exhausting and humiliating. That's why people flee from fitness centres like rats from the Titanic, while the garages and junkyards of the nation fill up with enough discarded home exercise equipment each year to provide the material, if it were all melted down, for a fleet of aircraft carriers.

Then comes guilt. Which can be appeased, during your working years, with the excuse that you have too many demands on your valuable time to make room for exercise. Once you retire that handy alibi is gone; you must face the naked truth and the unavoidable choice: fall into line or fall apart. I think that's one of the major reasons so many people keep putting off retirement.

For those who cannot bear the monotony of repetitive, stationary indoor exercise regimes there are always sports such as golf, curling and bowling. These have the added attraction of supplying some of the competitiveness, pursuit of material rewards, interpersonal conflict, mental stress and nervous exhaustion that you got used to during your working life and missed once you retired.

For those of us — and I am one — with a yearning for more solitary, less structured activity there are such things as back-country hiking, cross-country skiing and canoeing. These offer you a chance to fall back on your own resources and to get to know yourself — a frightening prospect indeed, and one which may well illustrate the maxim that ignorance is bliss. (See also **AGING, WEIGHT.**)

EYESIGHT.

The weakening, with age, of this sense is not always a bad thing. While "selective hearing" has long been noted with considerable amusement, there is definitely a place for "selective vision" as well, e.g. putting your glasses on for driving, reading or watching TV; leaving them off when the commercials come on or when checking yourself out in the mirror first thing in the morning. (See also **MIRROR, SPECTACLES.**)

F

FACELIFT.

As we age, various parts of our bodies begin to droop, sag and hang. Some of these parts can be hidden with careful choice of attire, but the face sticks right out there where everyone can see it. You could cover it with a ski mask, of course, but that could cause a bit of a stir when entering your local bank or convenience store.

Once upon a time grandpas and grandmas didn't seem to mind looking older, especially since small grandchildren found comfort, security and joy in the presence of those well-worn faces. But those grandpas and grandmas never saw 65-year-old celebrities with carefully manufactured 30-year-old faces in the media. Also they were not tempted by a vast array of multibillion-dollar industries offering to arrest the appearance, if not the essence, of aging.

Their remedies are of two general types: (1)Cosmetics of various kinds, including facial creams that "cleanse", "energize" and "feed" the skin. (Did you know it was dirty, lazy and hungry?) (2)The facelift. I'm a bit hazy on the technicalities, but I understand it's something like attaching the business end of a small crane to the skin at the top of the face and hoisting it up a notch or two at a time while loosening it from the underlying tissue, being careful not to cover over the appropriate holes for seeing, breathing and eating. Once the skin has been ratcheted up high enough it is tied securely over the ears and presto! Father Time has again — in the mind of the patient — been cheated. But look: the old boy's still grinning. He's very patient. (See also **HAIR, LIPOSUCTION, PLASTIC SURGERY, TUMMY TUCK.**)

FAMILY TREE. See **GENEALOGY.**

FANTASY.

The objects of your wildest dreams have no doubt changed over the years, going typically through the following stages: (1) all the ice cream and candy you could eat, (2) all the girls/guys you could desire, (3) all the money and status you craved, (4) a golf score under 85 and a top-of-the-line recliner.

FAQ.

These are the questions of most frequent concern to potential retirees. I should explain, to be fair, that the answers tend to reflect my own experience and inclinations.

1. Q. When should I retire?
   A. Tomorrow, if possible. (Yesterday would have been better.) If not possible, then at the earliest opportunity. (See **WHEN.**)
2. Q. How can I finance my retirement?
   A. In my experience just trusting to luck is the best bet. (My luck was to belong to a compulsory workplace pension plan with automatic premium deductions from payroll.) There are many other complex investment

schemes available from a variety of sources but they all require initiative, foresight, willpower and a lot of calculation, so I ignored them. If you can think of no alternative, however, see **FINANCIAL PLANNING.**

3 Q. How should I plan for retirement activity?
A. Professional consultants generally advise making elaborate plans for how to arrange your time after retirement. My question: If you want to have a full agenda, complete with pre-planning and scheduling, why quit working?

The best method, I think, is to wake up each morning, revel in the thought that you are not beholden to anyone or anything in particular, and then say to yourself, "Ah, what shall I do today?" Sometimes the answer may well be, "Nothing." (See also **LEISURE.**)

4. Q. But how will I keep from getting bored?
A. The only retired people who become very bored are the very boring.

5. Q. Where should I live after retiring?
A. Indoors, would be my suggestion. Beyond that, whatever suits your lifestyle. (For details see **DWELLING.**)

6. Q. What can I do about my health?
A. By all means, keep it, and take it with you when you retire. (But don't overdo the self-denial thing.) See also **DIET, EXERCISE, LONGEVITY, MODERATION, NUTRITION.**

FASHION.

Many aging people think that keeping up with current trends and fashions is a sign of being young at heart when it is really a sign of mindless conformity. Keep in mind what fashion really is: the spending of money you don't have to buy things you don't need to impress people you don't like. You don't have to do that anymore. So don't. (See **AGING, advantage # 1**; also **CLOTHING, COOL, TRENDS.**)

FIGURE.

If you once prided yourself on having the figure, depending upon your gender, of Venus or Adonis, but find you now resemble a geriatric Bacchus, don't despair. Retirement may provide you with some time to do something about it. (See **DIET, EXERCISE, FOOD, NUTRITION, WEIGHT.**)

FINANCIAL PLANNING.

Dreaming of retirement is one thing; trying to come up with a plan for financing it can be a nightmare. Some of the options are as follows:

1. The best method is to have a parent who is very rich, very old and has no other offspring. The beauty of this arrangement is that it requires no agent, no contributions and no planning. Its one drawback is, of course, painfully obvious.

2. The pension plan in which the employer deducts a premium from each of your paycheques and contributes a matching amount to your retirement fund is a perfect vehicle for young employees who have no intention of growing old and therefore have no

plan for that eventuality. I was once one of these. I was a teacher, and in my first years on the job I paid no attention to the speakers at conventions who explained how someone was making responsible arrangements for my future. This did not interest me because retirement was several hundred years in the future; in fact I rather resented the monthly premium deductions, feeling I could have used those funds more wisely for fishing tackle, records, beer and other vital necessities.

But a strange thing happened. The years began to pick up speed. Soon they were arriving and vanishing so fast that before I knew it, early retirement loomed just over the horizon. Now I began to think about it, and now I felt an overwhelming sense of gratitude to, and respect for, those serious gentlemen who had long ago tried to explain to me the mysteries of unfunded liability and the distinction between the formula plan and the annuity plan.

3. A big portion of my generation worked for government agencies or large companies most of our lives. Often our employers treated us much like family, specifically like somewhat slow-witted children whom they had to take care of with things like dental plans, insurance policies and pension programs. We lapped it up, and we gave a considerable amount of loyalty to our employers in return. Now, however, more people are self-employed or work for small businesses, and those who work for large organizations, private and public, have had to learn some new words — among them:

cutback, rationalization, re-positioning, downsizing — and have forgotten some old words, like loyalty. As a result those who are not self-employed expect to work for several different organizations in the course of their working lives, and most will have to depend upon their own initiative to make retirement plans. Which to me and many of my generation is like depending on the farmyard geese to come up with their own strategies against marauding foxes.

As to the various self-initiated investment strategies, I am reluctant to advise anyone, considering my own experiences in the field: I have made attempts at RRSPs (stands for Registered Retirement Something-or-other — mine was big enough when I cashed it in to support me for about a week), Savings Bonds (spent them long ago), life insurance policies that pay out on the date of maturity (cashed them in about twenty years too early), bank savings accounts (they stubbornly refused to grow on their own without regular contributions) and Guaranteed Investment Certificates (great in the days of high interest, when I was paying even higher interest on loans and mortgages and therefore could put very little into GICs, not worth a hoot now that interest rates are low and my borrowing days are pretty much over). My experience, in other words, has been as wide as the Mississippi and as deep as a backyard paddling pool. Better check with an expert.

If you have a business of your own you can sell it when you're ready to retire. If your transactional techniques resemble mine, however (my motto: buy high, sell low), forget it.

5. Armed robbery is lucrative, but risky, especially if you wait until late middle age before commencing this retirement plan. It would be inconvenient to have your back go out as you're making a fast getaway.
6. White-collar crime is physically safer than Option # 5, but more complicated. That's fine if you are a wizard with accounting procedures, but if your comprehension of fiscal affairs is similar to mine (I have trouble with the complexities of making out a deposit slip) this is not an option.
7. Buying lottery tickets to finance retirement is the choice of 11% of Canadian workers, according to a recent poll. This method has the advantage of being simple (in more ways than one), though it is not for the faint-hearted. (I hate to brag, but I was once involved in an even more daring scheme, where the odds are even steeper than in the lotteries: I was a partner in a farming operation.)

(See also **FAQ, HIGH-RISK INVESTMENT, MUTUAL FUNDS.**)

FISHING.

No doubt you will, as retirement looms, often hear the remark, "Lucky you, you'll have lots of time for fishing." Just why this is such a popular sport is not easy to determine. Perhaps because it combines relaxation with challenge. (Outsmarting an animal with a brain the size of a marble is apparently a proud achievement.) It may be the primitive satisfaction, like that found in hunting or berry picking, of wresting a basic need — food — directly from nature without having to pay for it (not counting the equipment, travel, boat rental and other minor expenses which usually amount to no more than $85 or so per ounce). Or, in the case of many males, it is an opportunity to get together with friends in sport and comradeship, drink truckloads of beer without being under the watchful eyes of wives, pee over the side of the boat, share dirty jokes and outrageous lies and stop shaving. (In my own case, of course, it is just the pure and simple pleasure of communing with nature.)

FOGEY.

A synonym (always preceded by "old") for old folk, old soul, old fart, geezer, gaffer etc., but with the added implication you are old-fashioned, uncool, and as obsolete as a Studebaker sedan. (See also **COOT, OBSOLETE, OLD-FASHIONED, WORD CHOICE.**)

FOOD.

For many people, as they age eating becomes less of a pleasure and more of a strategy. (See details under **NUTRITION. See also DIET, WEIGHT.**)

FORCED RETIREMENT.

When I came across this term in a retirement Web site recently I had to look twice. Some people have to be forced to retire? Apparently when some workers reach their employers' compulsory retirement age they resist. I don't get it. That's like a kid resisting ice cream on a broiling-hot day. A politician turning down an invitation to speak. A yuppy refusing to accept the BMW he won in a lottery. Of course I realize there are people who are less — "laid back", let's say — about working than I am, but do they have to be fanatics about it? (See also **ENERGY, LABOUR, WHEN, WORK, WORKAHOLIC.**)

FREEDOM.

Liberty. Independence. Escape from the restrictions and obligations of the workaday world. These are the Blessed States of Being that those approaching retirement look forward to so longingly. In my case the best time is when I awake in the morning to that delicious feeling of absolute freedom to do as I please with my time. It lasts about four minutes; then my calendar, my conscience and my wife remind me of the chores and responsibilities that have somehow laid claim to me since I retired. I suspect this scenario is common to most retirees, particularly in the first few years. Don't despair. Eventually your load will become lighter to accommodate the fact that your physical and mental faculties are deteriorating. Isn't that a comforting thought? Well, Fate is a cruel master. (See also **TIME, WORK.**)

FRIENDS.

One of the great pleasures of retiring is having more time for your friends. Especially treasure those who have known you since your youth: if they have put up with such an annoying, self-centred and wrong-headed individual as yourself for all those years and are still willing to associate with you they are gold indeed. Hang onto them. (See also **LEISURE, suggestions #1 and #2.**)

FURNITURE.

The smart retiree will decide that from now on, when choosing new furniture, status is out, comfort is in. My old easy chair may not be a sight for sore eyes, but it's a site for sore bones. (And an eyesore, says Guess Who.) See also **ROCKING CHAIR, SOFA**.

G

GAFFER. See **COOT, FOGEY.**

GARDENING.

One of the leading leisure activities of retired people. And I use the word "leisure" here very loosely indeed. Spending dozens of hours per week covered with sweat, dirt and carnivorous insects is not, to my mind, any reasonable person's idea of leisure. I know many people — my wife included — to which it is more like an addiction. One warning about these people: don't ask them how their gardens are doing. Not unless you have nothing important to do for the next hour except listen to detailed stories about how they valiantly outsmarted and conquered every fungus, weed and plant-devouring insect known to man. The traits of verbosity and the green thumb are located in the same gene. (See also **YARD WORK.**)

GEEZER. See COOT, FOGEY, WORD CHOICE.

GENDER DIFFERENCES.

We tread on dangerous ground here, as I have discovered to my sorrow when previously writing on this subject. Indeed most of the pleasures, problems and needs of retired and aging people are identical for both sexes. However, I cannot honestly avoid noting a few minor differences that exist — holdovers, no doubt, from the Bad Old Days before Enlightenment.

1. **FEMALE:** Desire for a retirement home that's neat, attractive and well located.
   MALE: Desire for a retirement home that's paid for.
2. **FEMALE:** Temptation to waste too much time watching TV soaps while overindulging on chips and chocolates.
   MALE: Temptation to waste too much time watching TV sports while overindulging on beer and pretzels.
3. **FEMALE:** While getting ready for an evening out, often becomes irritated with spouse for the carelessness of his appearance.
   MALE: While getting ready for an evening out, often becomes irritated with spouse for lateness of her appearance.
4. **FEMALE:** Tends to claim bragging rights on her children, grandchildren, hairdresser and new furniture, in that order.
   MALE: Tends to claim bragging rights on his children, grandchildren, new car and golf prowess, not necessarily in that order.
5. **FEMALE:** Those with growing waistlines tend to react by buying latest exercise gadgets advertised on TV or going on crash diet.
   MALE: Those with growing waistlines tend to react by chucking their belts and buying suspenders.
6. **FEMALE:** Spends considerable time dreaming up projects around the home for husband to

complete — after all, he's no longer working.
MALE: Spends considerable time dreaming up ways to avoid wife's projects — after all, he stopped working for a reason. (See also **CHORES, DOMESTIC HARMONY, HOME IMPROVEMENT, HOUSEWORK, MENOPAUSE.**)

GENEALOGY.

You may, like many retirees, decide to use some of your new-found time to search out your family history. Do not fear that you will discover pirates, outlaws, swindlers and other assorted scoundrels there; fear instead that you will find none of these, that indeed your ancestors were every bit as boring as you are.

GERIATRICS.

"Science of the diseases and care of the old." (Webster's) There you are: a whole new fast-growing field of science that will, in the not-too-distant future, be opening up to you! And you'll be right at the centre of it — like a rat in a laboratory. Isn't that exciting? (See **HEALTH, PHYSICIAN.**)

GOALS.

Ideally the whole concept of setting goals — which are troublesome and disruptive to the peace of mind — should be dumped once you retire. However this may not be possible; old habits are hard to break and you have been propagandized since childhood by teachers, coaches, bosses, motivational speakers, counsellors, writers of inspirational articles and various other annoying busybodies about the importance of setting goals. The idea of living in a state of unplanned spontaneity scares the hell out of you.

The trick is to replace your old goals (increase efficiency, boost sales, get that promotion at all costs, suck up to superiors, improve personal image, make co-workers look bad, retire at 55) with new ones (one-finger farewell to boss on last day, violent destruction of alarm clock next morning, two golf games per week, two hours couch time per day, four fishing trips per year, steak every Saturday).

GOLDEN YEARS.

Life after retirement: the Golden Years. Providing you have the gold, that is.

GOLF.

We can't discuss retirement without mentioning golf, the most popular activity, second only to gardening, of retirees. Most of my contemporaries are addicted to it. I, however, take seriously the old joke about golf being a sure-fire way to spoil a good walk. (That's assuming anyone who golfs ever walks anymore. The only exercise you get when using a power golf cart is getting on and off it.) Why, when out enjoying the sights, sounds and smells of nature, would you want your movements dictated by a small white ball?

When not out on the fairways, many of my friends are watching someone else play the game on TV. Personally, I find watching ice cubes melt more exciting. (Have I tried golfing, you ask? A few times. Was I any good at it? Well, my personal experience with the subject is not relevant here.)

GOOD OLD DAYS.

Were they really as good as they appear, or did they just seem so because at the time you were (a) younger, (b) often drunk, and (c) not yet burdened by many responsibilities? Or is it (d) because your memory cells have altered many of the details to suit your illusions? (See also **PAST, REMINISCENCE.**)

GOSSIP. See **CONVERSATION.**

GRANDCHILDREN.

Most people of retirement age have grandchildren. Most people of retirement age talk endlessly about their grandchildren, a topic which is dear to them, but which others often find boring. Unless, of course, the grandkids are truly remarkable children, like mine. (I had planned to include at this point a small photo and short biography of each of my eleven, but my editor — out of jealousy, no doubt — says no. Too bad, you would have been charmed and fascinated.)

One of the many pleasures of grandparenting is that you can often see in a grandchild some of the qualities which you possess. But the kid hasn't yet had time to misuse or fail to develop those traits; hasn't, in other words, screwed up the way you did. Thus you can supply him or her with valuable advice (giving advice becomes ever sweeter as you grow older) in avoiding the pitfalls you stumbled into. The beauty of the situation is that while young, the child will actually believe what you say, will look to you as a genuine source of wisdom. Enjoy that brush with idolatry; it vanishes at about age twelve.

"Look, Grandpa," one of my grandchildren once said, "that cloud looks like Fergie [our dog] chasing a ball." And by golly the kid was right. Let your grandchildren reawaken in you the ability you had as a child to find wonder in the commonplace. Might come in handy when you enter your second childhood. (See also **BABYSITTING, CHILDREN.**)

GRAVITY.

This phenomenon appears in two forms, both of which become more evident as you age:

1. Physical gravity: On this one you can blame the fact that (a) snow shovels, clothes baskets and shopping bags are all capable of carrying much heavier loads than they used to, (b) getting up from chairs and sofas requires much more effort than it once did, and (c) chins, cheeks (all four of them), breasts and bellies have begun a slow but certain southward migration.
2. Attitudinal gravity, i.e. "getting serious": Some people seem to believe that as they age it is appropriate to adopt a very serious manner and to condemn levity and lightheartedness. If you are one of these you should look in the mirror more often, especially when you are naked — it will remind you that Mother Nature has a sense of humour. (See also **DIGNITY.**)

GUILT.

One of the major obstacles, in a work-work society, to happy retirement. I have, however, some good news on that front, based on research I did for a recent column. I have often made fun in print of workaholics. (Do I perhaps harbour unconscious guilt at not being one? After all, workaholism is a trendy, high-status condition; just look at all the annoying celebrities who brag in the media about being addicted.)

Thus it was with satisfaction I recently read studies which indicate that (1) hours of work are increasing for many, even as technology takes over more tasks that once required human hands and brains, (2) high numbers of employees report feeling stress because of not having enough time for partners, families and favourite pastimes, (3) workplace time-stress is linked to higher consumption of cigarettes, fatty fast foods and alcohol as well as reduced exercise, (4) workplace stress may be a contributing cause of high blood pressure and cardiovascular disease.

What all this boils down to is the clear message: workaholism is bad for you. Bad news for workaholics. Good news for me. (See also **WHEN, WORK, WORKAHOLIC.**)

GULLIBILITY.

Now that you are in the "old hen" or "rooster" category (i.e. no longer a "spring chicken"), you have learned much, often from hard experience, about the hidden motives of your fellow humans, and are nobody's sucker. Until, that is, someone asks your age and, upon reply, says, "Oh surely not, you don't look that old," or, "Why you're the same age as So-and-so, but you look much younger." Was there ever a time you didn't believe that person, you old hypocrite? It has been said, in fact, that there are three ages: youth, middle age and "My you're looking good today."

H

HABIT.

By the time we reach retirement age most of us have adopted a few habits: good ones (regular housecleaning, thrifty buying, keeping informed of current affairs) and not-so-good ones (interrupting, frequent between-meal snacks, breaking wind in public etc.) The trick, we are told, is to substitute a good habit for each bad one. Chewing gum instead of smoking, for example. Personally, I plan to substitute twice-weekly basement cleaning for my habit of procrastination. But not right now. Maybe next year. (See also **SELF-IMPROVEMENT.**)

HAG.

Along with **CRONE**, this is the female equivalent of **CODGER, COOT, GAFFER** and **GEEZER**. Why there are more male than female terms for "silly old fart" I don't know, and don't really want to. (See also **FOGEY.**)

HAIR.

What most defined the Baby Boomers in their 1960s heyday? Free love? Rebellion against parents, schools, churches, governments and common sense? Clothing styles a circus clown or hobo would reject? The willingness to smoke anything that didn't run away? No. Most of all it was hair: long hair, wild hair, curly hair, straight hair, stringy hair, facial hair (on males, mostly), hair everywhere. Hair was the symbol of revolution, of rock music, of the New Morality, of all the Boomers stood for or against. The most successful musical production of the era was called . . . what else?

But as the Boomers age, their hair is betraying them. It's graying, it's receding, it's thinning, it's — in many cases — going, going, gone. So they drench it with shampoos, tonics, dyes, thickeners, conditioners, reconditioners, hot oil treatments — you name it. They attack it with specially designed combs, brushes, curling devices and blow dryers. And after drowning it, drying it out, burning it, boiling it and bombarding it with multitudinous forms of substance abuse, they wonder why it continues to deteriorate, while the makers of all those preparations and all that equipment chuckle and count their money.

If, however, you want to become fabulously wealthy, forget the high-tech stocks, forget oil, forget diamonds. If you can present Baby Boomer males with a sure-fire potion to grow hair on bald pates you'll be able to spend winters in your choice of Cuba, Jamaica, Bermuda or any other sun-drenched island nation, because you'll own them all. You'll never again have to worry about doing income tax returns; you'll just call up your nation's treasury department and ask them how much they need.

HARDSHIP.

Experiences of your past life that you hope to horrify and impress your kids and grandkids with, and look back on with pride, picturing yourself as a tough survivor. For my parents' generation it was World War and Depression. For my generation it was hard work on farms, in forests and factories with incomes which seem very inadequate by today's standards. For the Baby Boomers it was college courses with exams at the end of them and Lawrence Welk on TV. (See also **REMINISCENCE.**)

HEALTH.

See **DENTIST, FAQ** (#6), **HYPOCHONDRIA, LONGEVITY, MEDICINE CABINET, MENOPAUSE, NUTRITION, PHYSICIAN, SIGNS OF AGING.**

HEARING AID.

Many older folk are too proud to wear a hearing aid until some very disturbing incident forces the issue. Like almost getting run down by a car they didn't hear coming. Or not getting a free complimentary drink in the local bar because they didn't hear the offer. As the Baby Boomer generation — their ears battered by the Stones, Led Zeppelin and the like — reach their senior years, these little devices will become as common as hair dye and capped teeth. (See also **TECHNOLOGICAL CONFUSION.**)

HIGH-RISK INVESTMENT.

If you have a gambling instinct, a strong heart and a bold personality (or, perhaps, a personality disorder), you may consider adding this kind of investment to your retirement income strategies. I tried a form of it once on a pitifully tiny scale. I should have known better. I've never bet on a prizefight, a ball game or an election without losing. I have this strange power, you see. Politicians and team managers should pay me to bet against them and thereby jinx their opponents. Thus it was that many years ago when I was a partner in a grain farming operation (which raised hell with grain prices, of course), I put some money into canola futures on the suggestion of some friends who were doing very well with them. It was only $100, but that was enough to bring an abrupt downturn to the futures market that it didn't recover from for some time. (See also **FINANCIAL PLANNING, MUTUALS.**)

HILL.

The Hill is a metaphor you can't escape: life is a battle up the steep side of it, then you're over it, and inevitably you'll be under it. After you've become as old as the hills, that is. "Downhill" is a more schizophrenic term. Sometimes it's good ("We've completed the hardest part of the project; it should be downhill from here on"). Sometime it's not so good ("Our business has gone downhill since we had to quit advertising"). Personally I think there's some great scenery on the far side of the hill: see **AGING.**

HOBBIES.

See **ARTS AND CRAFTS, BIRD WATCHING, CAMPING, CARDS, COLLECTING, CURLING, FISHING, GARDENING, GOLF, LEISURE, SPORTS.**

HOLIDAYS.

The saddest thing about retirement is that there is nothing to take a holiday from any more. The first year I retired from teaching I got a sadistic charge out of watching the teachers and students go grumbling back to school in the fall. However, when they got out again in the spring I realized, with a pang of regret, that I would never again feel that exhilarating sense of release from toil. Almost made me feel like going back to work. But I got over it.

HOME IMPROVEMENT.

Many people see the time suddenly freed up by retirement as an opportunity to make the changes to their dwellings they have long dreamed of.

However, there is a gender difference which often shows up here. If you see a woman standing in the middle of a room, looking around in all directions, chances are she's thinking about moving the sofa to another corner, repainting a wall or knocking out a partition and installing new cupboards. If you see a man standing in the middle of a room looking around in all directions, chances are he's thinking: where the hell did I put my glasses? Or, where's that TV remote?

Maybe it's just me, but I could live in the same house from cradle to grave, if it's comfortable enough in the first place, and would feel no desire to make any alterations. I would not change the wallpaper until it fell off. I would never replace a rug until my feet started getting caught in the holes. Unless a ceiling fixture came crashing down on my head it would serve to light my way as well today as it did twenty years ago.

But whenever my wife Esther, looking up from her magazine at the wall or ceiling says, "Terry, you know, I've been thinking . . . ," I experience a sinking feeling, especially in my wallet. I have visions of total disruption, unnecessary labour, mess, chaos, possible bankruptcy.

I see a house as a home. Esther sees it not only as a home but as a gallery displaying various shapes and colours, a gallery, unfortunately, with constantly changing themes. (See also **DOMESTIC HARMONY, DWELLING, GENDER DIFFERENCES.**)

HONESTY.

No doubt honesty is the best policy — most of the time. It is a well-known fact, however, that aging people should, to preserve their physical and mental health, practise moderation in all things. And that includes honesty, which becomes a source of harm if overdone. Think about it: when your friend asks if you think she's holding her age well, are you really going to tell her you've seen fewer wrinkles on a circus elephant? Are you going to deprive your cronies of those fascinating and hilarious stories from your past by sticking too closely to the mundane details of what was actually a pretty boring life? What's the point? (See also **MEMOIRS, MODERATION, MORALITY, PAST, RELIGION, REMINISCENCE.**)

HOUSEWORK.

When both parents work it is only fair that both of them share the chores at home. When both are retired, then, it follows that the same rule should apply. That is logic at its plainest, against which there can be no reasonable argument, right? Of course. But it doesn't happen, does it?

Working or retired, the female does the bulk of the housework. The male, to assuage his guilt, argues that he is responsible for maintaining the vehicle (which means he washes it occasionally and phones the service garage for appointments; total time per year: six hours) and the house and lot (renail a fence picket or two, cut lawn once or twice, call roofer or plumber when necessary; total time per year: ten hours). His wife, meanwhile, does the cooking and cleaning and most of the yard work (total time per year: 850 hours).

In fairness, it is not only the male who is responsible for maintaining this traditional arrangement. The retirement advice columns are full of letters from women who are at their wit's end because their retired husbands are always underfoot, following them around and interfering with their household chores. I try not to bother my wife that way. At first she did expect me to help out around the house a fair amount, but it turned out I made so many mistakes that she had more work than ever making them right again and eventually forbade me to attempt any but the simplest tasks. (I know what you're thinking, but no, I didn't do it on purpose, really, I'm just a natural-born klutz.)

A recent University of Michigan study says men are doing more housework than they once did. American males do sixteen hours per week, up from twelve in 1965. Swedish males put in twenty-four hours per week. (Do you believe that?) Japanese men are the pikers — or the most honest — at four hours. There are no figures for Canadians, thank goodness. See also **CHORES, DOMESTIC HARMONY,**

GENDER DIFFERENCES, HOME IMPROVEMENT, RETIREMENT ADVICE.

HYPOCHONDRIA.

For the true hypochondriac the onset of advanced age is a true blessing. Why? Because something is bound to go wrong sooner or later and then (s)he'll be able to say, "See, I told you I wasn't well." In addition, hypochondriacs, once retired, will have more time to explain in greater detail every symptom of every ailment they claim to possess, to describe explicitly every treatment they've ever taken, to evaluate thoroughly every health professional they've ever seen. And they will find audiences for their complaints everywhere among other retired people, who have either become newly interested — because of their own infirmities — in things medical, or are no longer nimble enough to get away in time when they see the hypochondriac coming. (See also **HEALTH, LEISURE** — suggestion #4, **MEDICINE CABINET, PHYSICIAN.**)

I

IDENTITY.

You may be one of those who spent much of your younger life trying to "find yourself", to define your true identity. By now (retirement age) you should have discovered exactly who you are. Hope you're not too disappointed.

IDLENESS. See **LOAFING.**

IMPOTENCE.

Test your knowledge: The greatest fear of the male of late middle age is (a) World War III, (b) spiraling gasoline prices, (c) impotence, (d) people finding out about his impotence. The answer? Well, it depends entirely on whether you, personally, are having trouble with the old flag-raising ceremony. (See **SEX.**)

INDEPENDENCE. See **FREEDOM.**

INDISPENSABILITY.

Perhaps you are one of those who justify your reluctance to retire on the grounds that your business or workplace may suffer a decline or even a failure without your essential presence. Let me assure you, you need not worry on that account. Five years from now it will be plain to all and sundry that not only was your contribution not indispensable, it never really was all that important. Feel better already?

J

JOB.

The thing you must give up in order to retire. Not as easy as it sounds: most North Americans seem to have a love/hate relationship with their work. As one who has a special aptitude for not working, I was not burdened with this problem. If you, however, need an incentive to quit the rat race, see GOALS, GUILT, LEISURE, SEMI-RETIREMENT, WHEN, WORK.

K

KNOWLEDGE.

By now you have accumulated a vast store of knowledge. Now, what to do with it? If you're like me, much of it consists of such matters as the highlights of the 1954 World Series, the name of the highest mountain peak on each continent, or all twelve verses of the obsolete folk song "Nobody But a Logger Stirs His Coffee with His Thumb". Useless? Well, not if you play a lot of Trivial Pursuit. (See also **WISDOM.**)

L

LABOUR.

The enemy. For combat strategies see **LEISURE, LOAFING, WHEN, WORK, WORKAHOLIC.**

LECTURE.

An item for which the old adage "It is better to give than to receive" is especially true. And at your age there is no longer any reason to deprive yourself of the pleasure. (See also **ADVICE, CORRECTIVE CRITICISM, MORALITY, PREACHING, WISDOM.**)

LEISURE.

During your working life you were in constant competition to prove you could take on more responsibilities, accomplish more and bigger deals, work more quickly and competently, be promoted faster and earn more money than the next guy/girl. In retirement you will be in constant competition to prove you can travel farther to more exotic places, make better golf scores, catch more fish and have more fascinating hobbies and part-time business ventures than anyone else.

Why? Because you are a perverse, irrational, self-centred individual? Well, partly, but it's also because, brainwashed into a workaholic competitiveness as you were by Western society when you were gainfully employed, you cannot break the habit. You see the couch, the lawn chair, the book, the forest trail and other symbols of relaxed enjoyment as the trappings of sinful indolence. So, how do you unlearn the workaholic past and indulge in guilt-free relaxation?

1. Cut off all former friendships. Those people are as warped as you are and will forever be a corrupting influence.
2. Think of all the boyhood and girlhood friends you once knew who were expected to get nowhere, who were impractical, negligent, unambitious, idle and happy. Look them up, spend time with them, learn from them.
3. Spend more time with your grandchildren, the small ones in particular. Little kids are interested in the charming, the impractical, the bizarre and *seemingly* unprofitable phenomena of life, and are happy to let you share in their joyful meanderings.
4. Learn the art of hypochondria. There's no guilt in taking it easy if everyone — including you — thinks you're sick.
5. Start a petition demanding legislation to have all workaholics banned from the media and lecture circuits. Those who wish to indulge in their vile addiction in the privacy of their own homes will be allowed to do so (this is a democracy after all) but those who insist on promoting it in public will be incarcerated or exiled to Antarctica. Let them try to organize projects among the penguins.

6. Contribute to research which will locate the part of the brain responsible for the work ethic. Some day you may be able to have it surgically removed.

   (See also **ARTS AND CRAFTS, COLLECTING, FISHING, FREEDOM, GARDENING, GOLF, GRANDCHILDREN, HYPOCHONDRIA, LABOUR, LEISURE, LOAFING, PACE, RETIREMENT ADVICE, SPORTS, WORK, WORKAHOLIC.**)

LIBIDO.

As an aging male, is the quality that made you a young Don Juan done gone? Or showing up all too seldom? As an aging female, has the flame of desire faded to an occasional flicker? Despair not. With retirement, often, comes revival. For details see **SEX.** (See also **BED, IMPOTENCE, SIGNS OF AGING # 8.**)

LIPOSUCTION.

Quiz time. Liposuction is (a) an intense kiss, (b) a procedure used in plastic surgery, (c) the facial expression which accompanies the drinking of really dry wine.

The answer is (b). The way it works, as I understand it, is that the doctor sticks a needle attached to a vacuum pump into the unsightly bulges on thighs, bellies and bottoms, and sucks out the fat. Sounds like something you could do much cheaper at home. But don't, please, because (a) you could get infection, (b) you could miscalculate the depth and suck out, say, a kidney, (c) if home liposuction catches on, plastic surgeons will see their business reduced to the point where they will have to settle for Buicks instead of Mercedes. That would be very sad. (See also **FACELIFT, PLASTIC SURGERY.**)

LOAFING.

The foremost purpose of retirement. Many retirees don't like the term (I'm quite fond of it myself, both the word and the practice), as it is frowned on in our workaholic society and is often confused with another unattractive "L" word — a four-letter one at that. If you fear being caught "loafing", just explain that you are "storing up energy for the next task". That should satisfy your warped friends and acquaintances. (See also **LABOUR, LEISURE, WORD CHOICE, WORK, WORKAHOLIC.**)

LONGEVITY.

Every now and then our local papers report a birthday celebration for someone who is over 100 years of age. Of course the reporters quiz the celebrant about his or her lifestyle in order to come up with clues as to the keys to longevity. I have, for your information and benefit, neatly summarized the responses of several centenarians as follows:

1. Have a wide variety of interests.
2. Focus your time and energy on one all-consuming goal.
3. Marry for life and make family a priority.
4. Don't be afraid to raise a little hell.
5. Eat sparingly.
6. Eat heartily.
7. Avoid alcoholic drinks.

8. Have a couple of belts of whiskey (or glasses of wine or beer) every day.
9. Be placid and easygoing.
10. Be feisty and aggressive.
11. Be energetic and active; make every minute count.
12. Don't get too fixated on work; make room for plenty of rest and leisure.

Very enlightening, wouldn't you say? But the response I liked best came from a 107-year-old man who, when asked how he's managed to live so long, replied that he just doesn't stop breathing.

I know people who say they don't really want to live to their tenth decade and beyond. Others want to observe what's going on in our ever-fascinating world as long as possible. And some just get a charge out of outliving all the relatives who've been impatiently waiting for them to pass on and let go of their money and possessions.

M

MARRIAGE.

Though the divorce rates in North America are notoriously high, if you and your spouse have managed to stay together until retirement time, you'll probably continue to do so. This may be because you've learned to accept each other's faults and treasure each other's company after sharing so many good and bad times together. Or maybe you've just learned to tolerate each other, much like you've learned to tolerate a bad back and hair loss, and no longer have the energy to go through with the splitting-up process.

Then there was the couple who waited until they were 100 to get a divorce. They'd decided to stay together until all the kids had died. (See also **DOMESTIC HARMONY**.)

MATRONLY.

An adjective describing women of a certain age which is supposed to make them feel better than "middle-aged". But it doesn't, does it? (See also **DISTINGUISHED**, **VENERABLE**, **WORD CHOICE**.)

MEDIA. See **BOOKS, COMPUTER, TELEVISION**.

MEDICINE CABINET.

Remember when your stereo was the most indispensable piece of furniture in your house? (See also **SIGNS OF AGING # 1 and #7**.)

MEMOIRS.

I've read some very entertaining and fascinating memoirs — those of Winston Churchill come to mind — and I've also come across some real duds. Over the past couple of centuries many individuals have, upon retirement, looked back on their accomplishments, real or imagined, and felt such an urge to commit them to paper that they could not resist. Well, they should have — resisted, that is — in most cases. If you feel such an urge ask yourself — and answer honestly — whether the world would really care about your meagre achievements. If so, go to it. Otherwise don't inflict another tedious, ego-driven autobiography on humanity. (Mine will be out in about a year. Watch for it.)

If, however, you are determined to spill all, remember this: (1) It's not so much what you've done as how you tell it. (2) Knowing what to leave out is as important as what to put in — see **REMINISCENCE**. (3) The public would much rather read about someone who sometimes makes a fool of himself — and tells about it — than someone who is always infallible and always a winner. (That's why I expect mine to go over big.) See also **PAST**.

MEMORY.

I had something quite interesting to share with you about this topic; unfortunately I've forgotten what it is. (See also **AGING # 5, BRAIN CELL DETERIORATION, MENTAL AGILITY, NOSTALGIA, PAST, REMINISCENCE, SIGNS OF AGING.**)

MENOPAUSE.

A. FEMALE MENOPAUSE: It would be extremely presumptuous of me to attempt to provide any information or advice to women on this subject. I could as easily advise Bill Gates on marketing software. At any rate there are hundreds of books, magazines and other media devoted to the subject. Let me then make just one small suggestion to the husbands of the women who have reached that phase of their lives: Learn to recognize the symptoms of this condition, so that when they appear in your spouse you can make plans to keep the hell out of her way.

B. MALE MENOPAUSE: Unlike female menopause, which has been a hot topic for decades, male menopause was invented only a few years ago by male medical personnel who were jealous of all the attention and sympathy females get at this stage of their lives. After all, among the main symptoms listed (I looked them up on the Web) are "sore body syndrome" stiffness, weight gain, appearance of common diseases of aging, changes in libido and sexuality, and fatigue. Pardon me, but isn't this what we used to call "getting old"? (See also **SIGNS OF AGING.**)

MENTAL AGILITY.

Experts tell us that the mind does not deteriorate with age if we keep exercising it. One method they suggest is solving mathematical problems, some of which, like the following, are often printed in magazine articles on the subject: If a train leaves Point A for Point B, 1432 kilometres away, at a speed of 75 k/hr, makes seven 15-minute stops to pick up freight and takes on six tonnes of freight at each stop, every 1500 kilograms of which will slow its speed by four k/hr, how long will it take to reach Point B? At which point I say, let the damn brain cells die. I don't need them that badly.

Anyway, my brain gets plenty of exercise just trying to remember where I've put my keys. (See also **BRAIN CELL DETERIORATION, MEMORY.**)

MIRROR.

In the interests of emotional well-being, mirrors and weigh scales should be banished from the homes of retirees, according to some of my friends. I disagree. These items should be used every day in the interests of maintaining a proper sense of (a) proportion, (b) humility, (c) true worth, (d) humour.

MODERATION.

A good policy for aging men and women. Very few foods, drinks or activities will prove harmful if you don't overdo them. One should practise moderation in all things, and that includes moderation: too much moderation is immoderate. Therefore, as a therapeutic exercise, you should occasionally throw caution to the winds, give 'er hell and accept the consequences manfully (or womanfully if appropriate). See also **ADDICTION, ALCOHOL, FANTASY, NARCOTICS.**

MORALITY.

After decades of struggling with the perplexing questions of right and wrong you should now have settled on a moral code of your own. No doubt you have discovered that behaving morally is much easier now than it used to be. Why? Because you no longer have the energy to sin as enthusiastically as you once did. Also, though you may have been a Sixties swinger committed to agnosticism and the New Morality, you have noticed the Great Beyond moving a little closer and it scares the hell out of you. You don't want to screw up your balance sheet too badly, just in case.

Whatever the reason for your better behaviour recently, you probably think it has earned you the right to preach to your children and grandchildren on the subject of Immorality. And I have noticed, over the years, that the men and women of advancing years who speak out most sternly against Immorality are the ones who were the worst hellions when they were young. Well, why not? If you're going to lecture anyone about anything, it's best to know the subject first- hand. (See also **ADVICE, CORRECTIVE CRITICISM, HONESTY, LECTURE, PREACHING, RELIGION, WISDOM.**)

MOTOR HOME. See **DWELLING.**

MUSEUM.

Possibly you have found that museums are inexpensive, yet interesting places to visit, and quite enjoyable until you notice that a fair number of the antique artifacts are younger than you are. You didn't really expect to find them in a museum, since it seems you were just using them on a regular basis not long ago. (See also **ANACHRONISM, NOSTALGIA.**)

MUTUAL FUNDS.

One of the investment options often used for funding retirement (see **FINANCIAL PLANNING**). I think they got their name because often — and certainly at the time I write this — they are, for agent and client, mutually depressing. Actually, they represent the only "smart" financial decision I ever made. I bought a small package of them, at a friend's suggestion, and did very well on them during the 1990s. Then, while scraping together some money to buy a vehicle, I sold them, just before they began to decline at the end of the decade. I have been told this was dumb luck, but I know it was judicious timing. (See also **HIGH-RISK INVESTMENT.**)

N

NARCOTICS.

If you are a member of the Baby Boomer generation, you probably considered Pot to be one of the Holy Trinity, along with Peace and Love. Later, as you found new gods (Money, Status, Respectability etc.) which demanded all your time and effort, you abandoned the old ones. But once you retire and have more time on your hands the temptation may return. If so, see the **ALCOHOL** entry for expert advice. Also remember you may soon be addicted to a whole new set of substances, e.g. Calcium Pills, Preparation H, Arthritis Medication, Extract of Prune, Metamucil. (See also **ADDICTION, MODERATION.**)

NATURE.

We are told that such pursuits as bird watching, recreational walking tours, cross-country skiing and rock collecting are gaining in popularity as the population ages. Many seniors, obviously, are lovers of Mother Nature. Which seems rather strange when you consider what Mother Nature is doing to them. (See also **BIRD WATCHING, CAMPING, FISHING, GOLF.**)

NOSTALGIA.

As we age we feel an increasing sense of attachment to those old things that have been part of our lives for decades. Which is why most of us have stayed married to them, I suppose. (See also **ANACHRONISM, MUSEUM, PAST, REMINISCENCES.**)

NURSING HOME. See **DWELLING.**

NUTRITION.

The consumption of food and drink was, for centuries, a prominent part of the social fabric. It was central to hospitality, conviviality, conversation, family tradition, the celebration of life's milestones, and pleasure in general. Until now. Now it is simply one strategy in the campaign for longevity and a more fashionable appearance.

For most of human history and in most of the world today, getting enough to eat was and is a major worry. In the modern Western world the big problem is how to arrange to eat less, how to resist the temptation of food that is far too abundant, too appealing and too easily available. What a terrible burden! And for many, of course, the health concerns associated with nutrition become more of an issue as we age. Some nutritional tips for the middle-aged and beyond:

1. Avoid foods which contain fat, sugar, salt, cholesterol or taste.
2. Select high-fibre foods which are raw, undercooked and hard to chew. A general rule of thumb: if it tastes like cardboard it's probably good for you.

3. Alcoholic beverages actually have health benefits, as long as you don't drink enough to give you any pleasure.
4. Drink about three quarts of water before dinner. It will give you a "full" feeling, thereby dulling the appetite, and for the remainder of the evening you will be far too busy running to the bathroom to think about eating.
5. When eating out, go to the most expensive restaurant in town and order something pricey from the menu. Then say to yourself with every forkful, "This bite will cost me $2.75." You won't be hungry for long.
6. When eating at a restaurant, bring along two or three grandchildren under the age of six. If you don't see how that would curb your food consumption you haven't done it yet.

(See also **DIET, FOOD, WEIGHT.**)

OBITUARY.

The old joke about aging people checking the obituaries daily to see if they're in there is itself due for burial, but I once heard a convention speaker give it a new twist. He was from New York City, and he advised that if you find your obit in one of the tabloids there don't worry; they're not too reliable. But if you find it in the *New York Times* lie down; you're dead.

It's my belief that your obituary should be published when you are about twenty. That way it could be included in your resume. With a recommendation like that there's no job you couldn't get. (See **DEATH, EULOGY.**)

OBSOLETE.

Everything you like to read, watch, listen to, wear, eat, enjoy and are; clearly a case of unplanned obsolescence. (See **COMPUTER, FOGEY, OLD-FASHIONED, TECHNOLOGICAL CONFUSION.**)

OLD-FASHIONED.

When I was young this was a compliment often applied to young people and meaning "down-to-earth, unpretentious, dependable". Today it means "out-of-touch, uncool, unenlightened, obsolete" — an accurate description, in other words, of you and me, right? (See also **FOGEY, OBSOLETE, TECHNOLOGICAL CONFUSION.**)

P

PACE.

One-Minute Bedtime Stories is a book — a real one, I'm not kidding — for busy parents. It contains traditional stories, each in a 60-second format. Add a two-minute bath, a 30-second tucking-in and a half-second kiss and you can, in five minutes, get two kids to bed and be back catching up on work on your computer.

Some fast-food franchises now have express lanes, and others use a form of electronic billing that can trim 15 seconds off the average 131 seconds it takes to get served.

Because today's viewers are fast and fickle with the channel changers, TV commercials — and many of the programs — run on at breakneck pace. I find this so irritating that the "off' button is, to me, the most useful one on the remote.

These are just three of the many ways business caters to the Western world's urge to live in the fast lane. Well, I don't know about you, but as I grow older I find this preoccupation with speeding up the clock idiotic. On the contrary, I want to slow it down. Therefore I propose we seniors refuse to co-operate with the speed craze. Read — or better, make up — long bedtime stories for your grandchildren. They'll love it; they too want to slow down the clock, especially at bedtime. Choose a restaurant where you can have a leisurely meal and quiet conversation. Unless, of course, you have small children with you. Then you'd better go to McDonald's, where you can get it over with and get out in a hurry. (I'm not in favour of haste, but I'm not crazy either.) Shut off the TV and take a leisurely walk in the park, a hike down a rural road, or a cross-country ski trip. There you will see things that are moving slowly — birds, cows, clouds — or not moving at all — standing deer, trees, the moon — but are still interesting. You will hear things — coyotes howling, wind in the trees, distant thunder — that are not loud or hysterically paced but are good to hear anyway. Hard to believe, I know, but give it a try. (See also **LEISURE, TIME.**)

PAST.

As you grow older you will have weaker eyesight, poorer hearing, less energy, less endurance and less hair, but one thing you will have more of than ever before is Past. And it will become more important — and sweeter — as time goes by. Especially if you judiciously adjust it to fit your nostalgic illusions and self-image. All it takes is a little modification and selection of detail. (See also **GOOD OLD DAYS, MEMOIRS, MEMORY, NOSTALGIA, REMINISCENCE.**)

PERFECTIONISM.

If you are not perfect by now it's not likely you ever will be, is it? So give up. Relax. Enjoy your remaining years. Recent studies have shown that an obsession with getting everything "just right" is not always healthy; it may be an attempt to compensate for feelings of inadequacy and lead to frustration and unhappiness. I was delighted to hear this as I consider myself a bit slack in many ways and sometimes have felt guilty about it. I have a wide range of interests that never come anywhere near the level of expertise. And that's all right, apparently. Therefore I suggest that in retirement you take an approach that can best be summed up by revising a few old proverbs as follows:

- *If at first you don't succeed, try again. Later. If you still feel like it.*
- *A stitch in time makes life too predictable.*
- *Anything worth doing is worth doing in a half-assed sort of way.*
- *Practice makes boredom.*
- *Measure once, cut twice.*

Now don't get me wrong. There are situations that require something close to perfection. When I'm going under the anaesthetic just before a brain operation I don't want to hear the surgeon say, "Gee, I guess I should have studied up a bit more on this type of case, but what the hell, I'll give it a try." And I hope the pilot of the airliner I'm on got better than a C+ in navigation. I can think of one or two pursuits that even I am a bit fussy about. But perfection, like so many other things, should be practised in moderation. (See also **MODERATION.**)

PETS.

Research indicates that keeping pets helps us to live longer, heal faster, maintain lower blood pressure and cholesterol levels, and have a better chance of surviving a heart attack. Many people, after their kids have left the nest, transfer their parenting behaviour to a dog or cat, probably satisfying a need for nurturing in the process.

We Chamberlains are notorious animal lovers and treat our pets rather well. My brother-in-law once declared that if there's reincarnation he wants to come back as a Chamberlain dog. To which my daughter-in-law responded that that would certainly beat coming back as a Chamberlain wife. I try not to take offense.

PHARMACIST. See **MEDICINE CABINET** and **SIGNS OF AGING # 1 and # 7**.

PHYSICIAN.

No one loves retirees more than your physician does (though as time goes by the local undertaker will begin to look more fondly upon you too). There are six good reasons for this touching affection:

1. *Better patient attitude:* Once people retire they become more aware of the importance of their health.
2. *Professional interest:* There are a host of fascinating new procedures and products designed to slow down aging.
3. *Professional application:* Aging people tend to have more health problems than younger ones.
4. *Money:* Reasons 1 to 3, of course, result in more visits to the physician's clinic, which has a positive effect on his or her bottom line.
5. *More money.*
6. *Still more money.*

No wonder your doctor has more blissful dreams about you than your lovers ever did. And you have never been loved more thoroughly, all of you, from top (removal of cataracts) to bottom (hemorrhoid surgery). (See also **DENTIST, FACELIFT, LIPOSUCTION, MENOPAUSE, PLASTIC SURGERY.**)

PLASTIC SURGERY.

My grandparents never heard of plastic surgery. Old people were supposed to have wrinkles, age spots and leathery skin; these were badges of honour, testaments to years of stalwart endurance in the face of hardship. But the Baby Boomers, having invented the youth culture back in the 1960s, are determined to be the best-looking seniors ever and, finally, the best-looking corpses in the graveyard. Thus it is that throughout North America there soon won't be a middle-aged face unlifted, a tummy untucked or a backside unliposuctioned. (See **FACELIFT, LIPOSUCTION.**)

POLITICAL CORRECTNESS.

I once made what I thought was an innocent remark to my wife, teasing her for some silly little thing she had done, and using the phrase "just like a woman". We were in an elevator at the time, and several of the other passengers looked at me as though I had just broken wind. Probably you can relate to that experience. Having spent most of our lives in an era when freedom of speech was in fashion, many retirees cannot keep up with what the Thought Police now consider it to be unforgivable, if not illegal, to say.

Well, maybe it's true that once we have all learned to say "firefighter" instead of "fireman", "custodial personnel" instead of "janitors", "first nations" instead of "Indians" and "vertically challenged" instead of "'short", prejudice and discrimination will vanish from the face of the earth. But I doubt it. In the meantime, spare me the talk of "senior citizens" (i.e. old people), cars that are "pre-owned" (i.e. used), school courses that are "culturally sensitive" (i.e. watered down) and artists that have a "fresh, untutored" (i.e. childishly incompetent) style. I'm willing to make one exception, however: I would appreciate it if you would refer to those of us whose scalp growth is getting rather sparse as "follically challenged" rather than "bald". Sounds much better, doesn't it? (See also **WORD CHOICE**.)

POLITICS. See **POLITICAL CORRECTNESS, SOCIAL/POLITICAL SHIFT.**

PREACHING.

The right to unload upon any available ears the vast store of wisdom you have accumulated over the decades is one of the sweetest pleasures of growing old. And because you are growing old your listeners — particularly those related to you — are likely to hear you out respectfully as you lecture them on the sins of their generation and the priceless lessons learned, through hardship and struggle, by your generation. It is good for the soul to keep in mind, however, that behind that fixed look of reverent awe they are — while watching your lips move — busily making plans for the upcoming weekend.

I should add, however, that you should always practise what you preach. Case in point: When the European Union began refusing certain Canadian farm products I not only proposed a boycott of European goods, I personally resolved to buy no French champagne, Italian suits, British cars, Dutch beer, or videos of European movies. Some of my friends uncharitably reminded me that I don't like champagne, Dutch beer or European movies (I find viewing them about as interesting as watching nails rust) and that I could no more afford to buy a British car or Italian suit than I could the royal yacht Britannia. But how do they know all those shiny stickers I pasted onto entry forms for the Reader's Digest won't some day pay off and I'll become rich and develop a burning desire for these luxury items? Will I then give in and start buying them? Never! Well, not all of them, anyway. (See also **ADVICE, CORRECTIVE CRITICISM, LECTURE, MORALITY, WISDOM.**)

PREHISTORIC.

To your grandchildren, who assume you were there to see the glaciers retreat and the wooly mammoth walk the land, everything that happened before the invention of the CD player is prehistoric.

PRIDE.

A quality which changes with age. When you were young you were likely to derive it from your athletic ability, your attractiveness to the opposite sex, your capacity for hard work, and your competence in your occupation. Now it is likely to be invested in your grandchildren, the accomplishments of your children, your own past achievements and the wisdom you have gained from hard experience. All of which you are likely, in your own mind, both then and now, to have exaggerated shamelessly. (See also **DIGNITY, WISDOM.**)

R

READING GLASSES. See **SPECTACLES.**

REGULARITY.

When you were young, being a "regular guy" was pretty important. Still is, but for an entirely different reason. (Sorry if this expression seems gender specific, but my wife informs me that there was no parallel term, i.e. "regular girl", and that only males would come up with such a dumb expression anyway. So there.) See also **MEDICINE CABINET, SIGNS OF AGING.**

RELIGION.

Many of us remember our aged grandmothers and other elderly relatives praying, poring over their Bibles and other religious literature, and warning us of the great Judgement to come. We assumed they had always been pious and righteous and would have been astonished to learn that old Granny was actually quite a hellraiser when she was young. Will you and I, in similar fashion, start cramming for our Finals as we get closer to the Reckoning? Possibly. After all, letting go of our favourite transgressions will become easier as our fleshly appetites diminish. (See also **MORALITY, PREACHING.**)

REMINISCENCE.

The older we grow the more we look back, and by the time we're well into retirement reminiscing has become a major hobby. "If you haven't much future," one wit has said, "the past grows, and the longer you live the more past you've got." Even more fun is sharing your reminiscences with your kids, grandkids and other younger people, who, of course, always look forward with unbounded eagerness to hearing stories of your early life. Especially if you keep telling the same ones over and over again so they don't miss any of the impressive details, and especially if you keep reminding them how much tougher and more honest your generation was, and how things now are pretty much going to hell in a handbasket.

What makes this pastime so satisfying is that in the process of reliving the exploits of your youth you can do a better job of it than you did the first time. This is not to say that you lie — heaven forbid — but that the memory is, with aging, not always totally reliable. And that's perfectly normal (as well as convenient); no one can blame you for that. It is, after all, the principle that counts. If you didn't actually send the school bully howling home, as you said, well, at least you stood up to him for a minute or two, and didn't get beaten as badly as usual that time. If you didn't really lead the scoring on your high-school basketball team, you did make one sweet shot when it was needed. You may not have been quite the lady-killer or the femme fatale you present yourself as to your cronies on coffee row, but there was that time . . . well, you get the picture. A little creativity is as important to the storyteller as it is to any artist or performer. (See also **CONVERSATION, GOOD OLD DAYS, MEMOIRS, MEMORY, NOSTALGIA, PAST**.)

RESOLUTION. See **HABIT, SELF-IMPROVEMENT**.

RETIREE.

There is a common stereotype of the retiree as a balding, gray-haired, paunchy guy dozing in a hammock with a cool drink near at hand. But it would be as appropriate today to picture a slim, well-dressed, well-haired woman, playing tennis or piloting her SUV down the freeway en route to a meeting. Now there is nothing wrong with the new concept, but the stereotype should not be sniffed at either. My hammock is very comfortable, and could you hand me my beer, please?

RETIREMENT ADVICE.

You may have a shortage of money, a shortage of hair and/ or a shortage of energy when you retire, but one thing you need not fear is a shortage of advice. It's everywhere: in magazines (including those targeted to seniors), in newspaper and radio columns and in hundreds of websites and counselling services specializing in retirement. All these sources seem to assume that you will emerge, after a lifetime of work, like a newborn baby into the world of retirement with no plans, no hobbies, no leisure-time experience of any kind, no manual or intellectual skills, no financial strategies, no health knowledge, no life skills, no friends and damn few brains.

The sad part is, that seems to be true for some. The letters and call-ins to retirement columns and shows often back up the assumption that many of us are totally incompetent at not working. Women complain about retired husbands hanging around underfoot, following them around as they do their housework, and generally driving them crazy. Others complain that their lives seem meaningless without their accustomed workday tasks, that time drags on forever. Some have started drinking heavily, eating too much, watching too much TV. These are, of course, the same people who moaned when the alarm clock went off every workday morning, strove for longer vacation times and complained bitterly about their dictatorial bosses, unreasonable workloads and heavy responsibilities.

It is the curse of the human race, it seems, in weather fair or foul, to be ever dissatisfied. It's as though we always expect to be disappointed and in that respect we are seldom disappointed. (See also **GOALS, FAQ, HOUSEWORK, LEISURE.**)

ROCKING CHAIR.

For generations the rocking chair was the symbol of well-earned comfort for the retired and for elder folk in general. But in our present more hectic and workaholic age it is more often associated with those who are unproductive, complacent, purposeless and satisfied with their idle condition. Which is exactly how I want to feel when I'm enjoying mine. (See **FURNITURE, SOFA.**)

ROUTINE.

A blessing and a curse. One of the reasons most of us long for retirement is to break free from the chains of a routine that rules every minute of every day. As a schoolteacher my workplace was supplied with bells that told me when to start work, when to take a break, when to sit down, when to eat and when to go home. I came to fully empathize with Pavlov's dogs. But there is much evidence that many people, upon retirement, suffer from "routine withdrawal" — a sudden, panic-stricken realization that their workday and workweek routines had structured their lives for them and that now they are left alone to actually — God help them — make decisions for themselves.

The answer to this problem, I believe, consists of making up a daily/weekly routine for yourself which specifies times for physical activity, indoor chores, outdoor chores, hobby work, reading, watching TV, shopping, entertainment and so on, that you can use to keep from feeling at loose ends. But this routine must be so flexible that you can, as often as you wish, wake up in the morning and say to yourself, "Hey, you know that schedule we have planned for today? The hell with it. Instead let's . . . (insert a favourite activity here, now and then a downright decadent one)." See also **BOREDOM, CHORES, FREEDOM, HOUSEWORK, LEISURE, SPORTS, TIME, VOLUNTEERISM.**

RRSP. See **FINANCIAL PLANNING.**

S

SADISM.

If you have ever wondered who the cruelest sadists in history are, consider: have you experienced any of the following recently?

1. You always loved to party, but had to worry about work or looking after the kids the next day. Now you're free to party all night, but by eleven o'clock the idea of hitting the sack seems more appealing.
2. You always wanted to go on a fly-in fishing trip to a remote lake, or perhaps it was a shopping trip to New York, but could never afford it. Now you can, but discover that you would rather spend the weekend with your grandchildren.
3. For decades you yearned for a real hot sports car, but it wasn't practical for a family. Now there's just the two of you, but when you get to the car dealer's you find that what really catches your eye is a minivan. (Well, all the grandkids would fit into it with room to spare.)
4. You planned to "kick up your heels" as soon as you no longer had to keep up a "reputation" to please your bosses and co-workers. You'd show them. But when you retired you found that (a) your heels won't kick very high any more (arthritis) and (b) no one cares

what an old fart like you does anyway. And that's no fun.

All of which proves that Mother Nature and Father Time are the most sadistic old pair on the planet. (See also **ADDICTION, SIGNS OF AGING.**)

SCAMS.

Yes, there are many scams directed at seniors, who, the scam artists seem to think, are (1) feeble-bodied, (2) feeble-minded, (3) lonely and craving attention, and (4) have a few bucks stashed away. If that describes you, look out. But even if it doesn't, avoid being attracted to offers via phone, mail, e-mail or door-to-door reps that promise fantastic returns on investments, prizes that require stiff fees to collect, miracle remedies for the symptoms of aging or rare merchandise at cut-rate prices. If you really want to get rid of your money, gamble or drink it away; at least you'll have more fun disposing of it. Or, if you consider it immoral to spend your surplus funds on drink and gambling, send it to me and I'll do it for you. (See also **GULLIBILITY.**)

SECOND CHILDHOOD.

Something to look forward to — after all, you should be able to do a better job of it than you did the first time around, because you'll be bringing a lot more experience to it.

SELF-IMPROVEMENT.

In January, 2000, I wrote a column in which I looked back at my New Year's resolutions for 1999 to see how well I had kept them. My comment on one of them: "I had . . . in view of my growing forgetfulness, resolved to take a course in memory improvement. Now I may have come through on that one and actually taken such a course, but I can't remember for certain if I did." And my one resolution for 2000: "To make no more resolutions."

Resolutions are for those who are not yet perfect. And while I don't pretend to be 100% perfect (I'm sure I could think of a fault if I had time), I'm too old now to make any more changes. Now there you have one of the beauties of growing old: it is now appropriate, is in fact expected of you, to be "set in your ways", thus you no longer need bother to make resolutions at New Year's or any other time. If, however, you are one of those terminally conscientious people, bent on self-improvement, you can go ahead and make those solemn commitments, secure in the knowledge that in no time at all you will have forgotten about them and can carry on with your comfortable old faults and habits. However, if you do persist in your addiction to personal reform, please don't come to my house; I don't need any more annoying people around me. (See also **HABIT, MEMORY.**)

SEMI-RETIREMENT.

Much like retirement, but enjoys a much higher social status. You must never, you see, unless you are at least ninety years old, tell anyone you are retired. The reply, with wrinkled nose and raised eyebrow, will be something like this: "Really? Gee, I can't imagine not doing anything all day." This remark implies, of course, that he or she is a person with energy, vigour, ambition and pride, while you are a poor, dull, weak-spirited creature, lacking in vitality and character.

Instead, say you're semi-retired. This implies that you're not really going to seed; you still have a finger in the workaday world as well as a host of leisure-time activities. Then put your smug listener on the defensive by asserting that you are self-motivated; you control your own schedule and can no longer imagine what it's like to slavishly allow someone else to set your agenda.

Now, what must you do to justify the semi-retirement label? Practically nothing. The term implies, of course, that you are still getting paid for something you actually do. (Walking out to the mailbox to pick up your pension cheque doesn't count.) Thus if you have a hobby, woodwork for example, and sell a couple of wooden lawn leprechauns a year, that qualifies you as semi-retired, even if you spend 98% of your time as a couch potato. (And now you know why I wrote this book.)

A word of warning: I have known a retiree or two who got into a tiny sideline business to earn the semi-retired designation, found it more lucrative than he had expected and expanded it until it completely took over his life. That's like finishing your prison sentence one day and doing something stupid enough to land you in jail the next. Don't let it happen to you. (See also **WHEN, WORK.**)

SENILITY. See **SECOND CHILDHOOD.**

SENIOR CITIZEN.

One of those oh-so-sensitive weasel words so popular in recent years. Well I hate political correctness, and I don't intend to be a Senior Citizen. I intend to be an Old Man. And a rather grumpy one too. (See also **DISTINGUISHED, SENIORS' DISCOUNT, VENERABLE**).

SENIORS' DISCOUNT.

Though I dislike the word "senior" when applied to old people (see **SENIOR CITIZEN**), I'll embrace it heartily when followed by the word "discount". The seniors' discount is — like grandchildren, personal freedom and afternoon naps — one of the great blessings of retirement. Its only negative aspect is when you're still in your 50s and a young hairdresser or teenaged waiter — to whom anyone with a few strands of gray hair is elderly — asks if you qualify for the discount. Ouch. Somehow the chance to save a buck or two then seems like a hollow gain.

SEX.

An active sex life, the medical experts tell us, contributes to good physical and mental health and may help to slow down the aging process. Well now, isn't that just great? When you were young and full of desperately raging, yearning hormones, you were ordered and advised by all adult authorities to restrain them. Now that those same hormones are considerably restrained by nature you are advised to get all you can. Go figure.

Apparently the frequency of sexual intercourse increases slightly when retirement begins. This is thought to be due to relaxation of the tensions that the workplace engendered. The real reasons, I suspect, are (1) as we age we tend to prefer stay-at-home activities to going out, (2) income is usually reduced upon retirement, and (3) television becomes very tiresome after a while. In other words, sex is readily available, cheap, and less irritating than the current crop of TV sitcoms (and probably funnier). See also **BED, IMPOTENCE, LIBIDO, SIGNS OF AGING # 8, SLEEP.**

SIGNS OF AGING.

In addition to symptoms mentioned in various other entries in this book, the twelve surest signs of aging are as follows:

1. Your medicine cabinet has filled to the point you're considering installing a second one.
2. You become more forgetful.
3. When you enter a strange room you check out the chairs before you sit down and try to figure out which one will be easiest to get up out of.
4. You tend to become rather forgetful.
5. You win tickets to a sporting event or concert and check them to see if it will be over before your bedtime.
6. Various parts of your body find ways to remind you it's time to arrange for maintenance.
7. Your pharmacist can't conceal her delight when you walk through the door. (Maybe she can send her son to a better college after all.)
8. When you mention that you've just had a "hot night under the sheets" everyone knows you mean your air conditioner is on the fritz again.
9. Though you are sure the winters are nowhere near as severe as they were 40 years ago, packed snow is

slipperier than it used to be and a shovel full of it is heavier.

10. The gray-haired folk with lined faces that you meet on the street are no longer your dad's childhood buddies. They're *your* childhood buddies.
11. The first thing you do upon entering any building is check out where the bathrooms are.
12. You tend to become a bit forgetful.

There are as well some rather positive aspects of the aging process, listed under **AGING**. (See also **ADDICTION, HILL, SADISM, YOU'RE OLD WHEN . . .**)

SLEEP.

The second most popular bedtime activity — though it creeps closer towards first place as you reach retirement age. In fact you probably look forward, as I did, to sleeping in a lot when your working life is done. I even planned, for the first few days of retirement, to set my alarm for the usual workday time, then sneer at it, shut it off, turn over and go back to sleep with a self-satisfied grin on my face. But you know what? I wake up and get up as early as I ever did — often earlier. And many other retirees have told me it's the same with them. I think Mother Nature is reminding us we were designed to get up and do things. (She can be a rather perverse old broad.) See also **BED**.

SMOKING.

Back in Paleolithic times, when I was young, we pictured the retired man (women never retired then) as rocking contentedly in his favourite chair, the smoke from his pipe curling lazily around his head. No more. The politically correct lobbies have made the pipe an object of fear and loathing, totally unacceptable to 21st century sensibilities when filled with tobacco (hashish and marijuana are somewhat more acceptable).

SNOWBIRDS.

Name for Canadian or Northern US residents — usually retired — who flee like self-indulgent cowards each winter to the tourist traps of sunny southern lands, ignoring the rich variety of enjoyable winter activities (for those not afraid of a little snow) right near their homes. (No, I can't afford to go. How could you tell?) See also **WINTER.**

SOCIAL/POLITICAL SHIFT.

It's been a well-known phenomenon for generations that people often become more conservative in their views as they grow older. But for the earliest wave of Baby Boomers, those who came of age in the 1960s, and many of whom adopted very "anti-establishment " attitudes, the shift has been especially striking. The New Morality (Art Uncensored, Toleration of Anything etc.), they discovered, didn't really suit their vision for their own children. Free Love and Unrestrained Sexuality didn't look so cool when their daughters began to reach adulthood. Taking more from the Rich to help the Poor didn't seem like such a clever idea once they began to accumulate property. When they were young they resented the taxes and premiums they had to pay to support old age pensions and other seniors' benefits, but suddenly those payments look like a pretty good idea, very fair compensation for all the wonderful things the

Boomers did for the generation that followed them. They learned as they aged, you see. And the generation that's now the same age they were then — what do those young whippersnappers know? (See also **POLITICAL CORRECTNESS, VALUES, WHIPPERSNAPPERS.**)

SOFA.

A piece of furniture most of us have looked forward to spending more time on once we dropped out of the rat race. Go ahead, enjoy it, but don't — like some of my retired friends — get too attached to it. (If you find yourself kissing it goodbye every time you leave the house, that's not a good sign.) See also **FURNITURE, ROCKING CHAIR.**

SPECTACLES.

I have known a few persons of both genders in my age category who refused for years to wear spectacles due to vanity. Often they made spectacles of themselves as a result — saying "Warm, isn't it?" to a department store mannequin, for example. Many of these same individuals now worship at the shrine of the inventor of the contact lens. One drawback: getting down on arthritic knees to search for a contact lens on the floor is difficult and frustrating, especially when you can't see a damn thing.

Most people my age know, as I do, from experience, that spectacles have a secret ability to migrate of their own accord when no one is looking, usually to a place of hiding. I have four pairs of reading glasses about the house and on several occasions not one pair could I find, they all having crept away to some unlikely spot. The first inventor to come up with a practical pair of "homing spectacles" — ones that will come when you call them or whistle or something — will be a shoo-in for a Nobel prize. (See also **EYESIGHT, TECHNOLOGICAL CONFUSION.**)

SPORTS.

When you were younger you no doubt played some sport — hockey, tennis, golf, whatever suited your energy level, and that could range from mountain climbing to billiards. You may cling to one or more of these for a time after retirement, but the day will come when even billiards may seem a bit too active. If you then still long to satisfy your competitive spirit you may wish to take advantage of the following list, which I have developed for your benefit.

SPORTS FOR THE OLDER RETIREE:

1. **REMOTE RACING:** Place the TV remote on the set, then sit down with your spouse on the sofa. At a previously agreed-upon signal (e.g. the start of the next commercial) you both get up and run (or walk, or limp) toward the remote. First one to get there can choose the channel.
2. **SLEEP MARATHON:** You and your spouse retire to bed at the same time. First one to wake up has to get up and make the coffee.
3. **FOREIGN FILM WAKEATHON:** Put a foreign film, complete with subtitles, on the VCR. Then you and your spouse, or a group of your age contemporaries, sit down and watch it. Last one to fall asleep gets to take whatever share he/she wants of the available junk food.

4. **PREVARICATION TOSS:** Host, hostess and friends of contemporary age sit around a room drinking martinis. Each tells a story from his or her youth. A vote is taken as to who has exaggerated and/or lied to the greatest degree and the others then pelt the culprit with the olives from their drinks.
5. **PILL ROLL:** Self-explanatory, except that either distance or accuracy or both can be included in the scoring. The winner gets a free jar of Metamucil, paid for by the losers.

Let the games begin.

STANDARD OF LIVING.

Most of us will experience a reduction in our income when we retire. That occurrence can be viewed as an opportunity to concentrate on appreciating the simple pleasures, to develop our inner resources, to learn to value human relationships above material advantages.

OK, when you stop laughing you can check out the information under **FINANCIAL PLANNING** to find out how to maintain your present disgusting level of affluence, self-indulgence and shallow existence.

STATISTICS.

Is it just me, or do most people, as they grow older, become more fascinated by statistics? I'm not sure why this is, because most of these number-crunching exercises — the increasing incidence, with age, of memory loss, cardio-vascular problems and various other conditions, for example — are not particularly encouraging. But now and then a very pleasing stat comes along. You have probably noticed, in other parts of this book, that I am waging an ongoing campaign against the dreadful curse of workaholism. Well, a recent Trade Union Congress report has given me deadly new ammunition. It reveals that Britons work longer hours than continental Europeans but get less done. The French, for example, are limited by law to a thirty-five-hour work week, but are 24% more productive, on an hourly basis, than the British, who work an average of 43.6 hours per week. Now you know how I hate to say "I told you so," but there it is.

I can only conclude that with statistics, as with sharing stories of one's past, it's best to be selective. (See also LABOUR, WORK, WORKAHOLIC.)

T

TECHNOLOGICAL CONFUSION.

If you, like me, can remember a time before television, before jet travel, before cruise control, before velcro, before nuclear weapons, before stereo and before communications satellites, and if, just as you were getting used to those things you found yourself bombarded with digital phones, personal computers, talking cars, video games, CDs, VCRs, DVDs and GMOs, then you have probably gone around for the past couple of decades in a sort of foggy daze, one desperate question on your troubled mind: what the hell are they going to do next?

Making use of these wonders, for those of us whose technological learning curve ended about 1965, is a challenge indeed. I can record a program on the VCR and play it back later (I am pathetically proud of that), but setting it to record something later, or getting it to perform any of the 40 or so other functions it is capable of, is a lost cause. The instruction booklets for these gadgets are a big help, of course — they are printed in about eight languages, none of which I speak, though one bears a faint resemblance to English.

Of course, as the Baby Boomer generation — which sacred fellowship I precede by a scant but hopelessly non-inclusive eight years — continues to reach retirement age, industrial technology will more and more cater to the aging consumer, adding continuously to such current blessings as the electronic hearing aid, the trifocal, the plastic hip joint and the TV remote. (See also **COMPUTER, OBSOLETE.**)

TELEVISION.

A major comforter, solace, sedative and (sometimes) narcotic for the aging retiree. I am one of those who has often proudly, virtuously and righteously expressed my disdain for the medium as trend-driven, mind-numbing candy for the brain. We get only two channels at our house, the only one of our circle of friends and relatives who don't get 50 to 400 channels via cable or satellite dish. We have always justified this on the grounds that 50 X Garbage still equals Garbage. Also we're cheap. However, having observed, when visiting our children, that several specialty channels seem to cater to our particular interests, we are considering a dish. We don't plan to tell our friends and relatives, of course, and we're not sure whether we're making a rational decision to utilize the benefits of modern communications technology or if we've just accepted the fact that our brain cells are deteriorating with age anyway.

One sure sign of aging is that you will sometimes find me laughing uproariously at episodes of "Green Acres" and "All in the Family" (my sons sometimes tape these antiques for me), but I sit confused in front of modern sitcoms, wondering what I'm missing, and feeling no urge to come up with a weak grin, let alone a laugh. Like Shakespeare's

Hamlet, I feel "the time is out of joint." Weren't comedies once funny instead of being showcases for displaying smart-mouthed kids, lifestyle fads, sexual innuendoes and lessons on political correctness? Am I sounding grumpy? Well, I am, and that's another sign of aging, so let's drop the subject.

TIME.

Most people complain (or is it bragging?) about living in the fast lane. More than half of working men and women, according to a recent survey, never have enough time for family, friends and personal interests. Almost half of them say they "often" or "almost always" feel overwhelmed by stress. Finally they retire, the rat race is over and they can enjoy a more leisurely existence, right?

Well, no, not really. According to the letters to retirement columns, the calls to retirement advice shows on radio and conversations I have with retired people, one of the biggest problems is that time passes too slowly; they can't fill up their days! As a result, some retirees become couch potatoes, hoping the TV will accelerate the march of time, while others plunge themselves into such frenetic activity that their working lives, in hindsight, were leisurely by comparison. Neither group is satisfied. The human being is a perverse species.

Fortunately there's professional help available — see **RETIREMENT ADVICE.** (See also **FAQ, FREEDOM, LEISURE, PACE, WORK, WORKAHOLIC.**)

TRAVEL.

A prediction: the minute you announce your impending retirement, half your co-workers will remark, "Now you'll have more time to fish," and the other half will say, "Now you'll have more time to travel." Indeed there are many benefits to traveling: (a) It is, as they say, "broadening" (especially if you go by car and eat often at fast food joints). (b) It makes it impossible to feel guilty about neglecting chores, as you would if trying to relax at home. (c) It makes it difficult for annoying relatives to catch up with you.

You can choose, of course, from among several methods of transport, each with its own set of experiences, advantages and disadvantages:

1. Hitchhiking: The least expensive method. You probably did some hitchhiking as a youth, but aren't likely to now. Which is ironic, especially if you are a male, because the drivers who didn't stop then because they had some fear of inviting a young, strong, perhaps long-haired and bearded person into their vehicles would now be quite willing to pick up a harmless-looking old coot like you.
2. Car or RV: In one of these you can experience, as you never could with mass transportation, (a) a more intimate relationship with the places you pass through and the people who live there, (b) highway accidents, (c) vehicle breakdowns, (d) getting lost.
3. Bus: Provides the experience of (a) travelling without having to drive, (b) not having to decide — someone else will — when and where to eat, when to sit down,

when to stretch your legs etc., (c) mingling with other travelers (a mixed blessing indeed).

4. Train: Same as bus, but not quite so restrictive and there's a bar.
5. Air: Similar experience to that of bus or train, with the added advantages of (a) speed, (b) ability to leave the continent if you so choose, (c) airline food (after which you'll never complain about your spouse's cooking again), and what I like best about air travel: (d) you never have to stop to ask for directions.
6. Ocean cruise: The one method I can't comment on with any authority, my budget being in the rowboat, rather than the cruise ship, category.

(See also **AUTOMOBILE.**)

TRENDS.

One of the blessings of retirement is that you can shed, along with stress and overwork, the need to be trendy. If you still, at this age, feel the need to impress others with your trendiness, that's very sad. Now is the time you can actually be yourself. (Though for some of the people I know that could be pretty sad too.) See also **COOL, FASHION. TUMMY TUCK, PLASTIC SURGERY.**

U

UNDERTAKER.

The physician, the plastic surgeon, the optometrist, the pharmacist and the dentist all have cause to smile, even chuckle, when they view the statistics which show that our general population is aging. But the undertaker will have the last laugh.

VALUES.

In your youth, and particularly if you were a Baby Boomer, it is likely that Innovation, Libertarianism, Candidness, Diversity and Anti-materialism were among the values you cherished. Later, as you entered the working world, these were gradually replaced by Perseverance, Diligence, Industry, Ambition, Acquisition and Status. And now you are more concerned with Security, Stability, Dependability and, of course, those values so vital to the well-being of many retirees: Stock Values. (See also **SOCIAL/POLITICAL SHIFT.**)

VANITY.

One of the burdensome vices which, by now, you should have conquered and left behind. Which shouldn't be difficult now that you have so much less to be vain about than you once did.

VENERABLE.

Another of those adjectives, like "distinguished", which is intended by younger people as a compliment. But it makes you feel about as flattered as if you had just been declared a National Historic Site. (See **DISTINGUISHED, MATRONLY, WORD CHOICE.**)

VOLUNTEERISM.

One thing you will discover soon after you retire — sure as varicose veins and misplaced spectacles — is that you will be approached by various groups to contribute volunteer service. If you played a leadership role in your working years you may well wind up doing the same for some non-profit organization. That way you can retain most of the conditions of the workaday world you would otherwise miss: regular time schedules, financial concerns, heavy responsibility, long meetings, interpersonal conflicts, mental and emotional stress. The only difference is you won't get paid. And if you don't get paid for doing good, does that mean you're good for nothing?

If this sounds like I'm knocking volunteerism, please don't take me seriously. Heaven forbid. Of all the retirees I know, those who put a lot of time into volunteer service tend to be the happiest, the most contented and the most youthful in outlook. As a confirmed lover of loafing I hate to admit that, but it's true.

WEBSITES.

Checking out websites on the subject of Retirement, you are soon led to believe that everyone approaching retirement is terrified of (a) going broke, (b) getting sick and (c) being bored. What a bummer. For more positive assistance see **FAQ, LEISURE, RETIREMENT ADVICE.**

WEIGH SCALE. See **MIRROR, WEIGHT.**

WEIGHT.

Not only are you likely, as you reach retirement age, to become more tolerant, more easygoing and more accepting of others — in short, more loveable — but there will probably be more of you to love than there ever was before.

To the Boomer generation that invented the youth culture, that's a big problem. But not everyone is upset about it. Those whose fortunes depend on courting the Boomers (and that's most of the economy) love every ounce of extra fat each one of them carries. They supplied Mr. And Mrs. Boomer with all the labour-saving devices anyone ever wanted, gave them comfortable and luxurious cars, provided them with expensive stereo and TV units to sit in front of (complete with remote controls), settled them on the most stylish and comfortable furniture ever made, catered to their palates with the most luscious entrees, the richest and most delectable desserts, the tastiest junk food any generation ever enjoyed.

Then, as the Boomers' bodies inevitably swelled to gigantic proportions under those conditions and they began to worry about it, there stood Industry again, offering the resources to take off what it had arranged for them to put on. Fitness centres, gymnasiums, diet books, diet plans, weight-loss drugs, low-fat processed foods and a bewildering array of weightlifting machines, rowing machines, exercise bikes, treadmills, tummy toners, thigh thinners, butt trimmers and more, at your service, on demand — for a price, reasonable and otherwise.

As the old hippies and aging yuppies approach the end of their working years they will, of course, be warned in a thousand TV commercials, newspaper ads, magazine spreads and billboards that the inactivity attending retirement could induce weight gain and threaten their health. They will be further informed that there are, however, products that can save them from such a fate. And they will buy those products. By the truckload.

Love those Boomers. What would our economy do without them? (See also **DIET, EXERCISE, FOOD, NUTRITION.**)

WHEN.

The biggest word in the prospective retiree's vocabulary. When is the right time to retire? For me the answer was easy: at the first possible minute I could. (Or thought I could; financial considerations kept me working a bit longer.) For many of my contemporaries it was a more difficult decision, one which some of them put off for years. They actually expressed a fear of retiring, felt they would be lost without the structure their work imposed on their days. Imagine that: prisoners in love with their chains!

The trouble, you see, is that we North Americans have turned work into a religious ritual. It's the chief ingredient of our identities. We feel guilty if we're not doing it. And to reinforce that attitude we have those creatures called workaholics on TV and in the newspapers and magazines bragging about how addicted they are to their work. I mean, they're actually proud of working all day and half the night seven days a week. They expect to be honoured for it when in fact they should be pitied, or, better yet, executed.

If you happen to be one of those who feel that your self-worth is irreversibly bound up with work I have two thoughts for you. First thought: You poor schmuck. Second thought: that's why God invented semi-retirement. (See **SEMI-RETIREMENT**, also **FREEDOM, GOALS, GUILT, LEISURE, WORK, WORKAHOLIC.**)

WHIPPERSNAPPER.

Anyone who is (a) at least ten years younger than you are and (b) has not yet accumulated the vast store of wisdom that you have. Whippersnappers need to be "tuned in", and you're just the guy (girl?) to do it. (See also **ADVICE, CORRECTIVE CRITICISM, WISDOM.**)

WILL.

Those who are provident, conscientious and responsible will have made their wills decades before retiring. The other 85% of us will begin thinking about it around the same time we start thinking about retirement. It seems people put off will-making because they don't want to face the prospect of their own deaths. Well, I don't know about your hometown, but in mine the death rate is 100%. Get used to it.

It's all a matter of attitude. Making a will can be fun. Where else can you get the chance to punish and reward as you please? To let your sister Gladys know you appreciate what she did for you and confirm for your nephew Morton that you are aware he is a no-good bum and deserves what you left him — nothing. If you like you can even impose some real cute conditions on your heirs — George, the swinging bachelor, can't get his share until he marries; Shirley, who hates your guts, has to name her firstborn after you. Talk about the last laugh! (See also DEATH, EULOGY, OBITUARY.)

WINTER.

If you're anywhere near my age, and if you hear people complaining about the weather in January, then you no doubt feel compelled to inform them that winters nowadays are nothing compared with the ones we used to put up with. In those days it was so cold we had foot-long icicles hanging from our noses, we had to climb over twelve-foot snowdrifts on our way to school, and we had ten-day blizzards at least once a week. Yet the winters were even worse, according to my dad, when he was young, and my grandfather used to tell me they were still worse in his youth. He recalled that after one fierce 19th century blizzard in the Dakotas whole herds of cattle were found frozen standing in the snow, as was one woodcutter, his axe poised above his head. Present-day winters are sissy things by comparison. Enjoy them before they become altogether extinct.

Yet strangely enough, many of my contemporaries who brag about how severe the old-fashioned winters were complain that they now feel the cold more and find the snow increasingly difficult to shovel. Just an excuse, perhaps, to flee south for a while. (See also **DWELLING, SNOWBIRDS.**)

WISDOM.

One of the supposed attributes of advancing age. Younger people (once they reach 30 or so and begin to realize their own generation isn't really the cleverest one in the history of the world) often assume you possess great wisdom because you have (1) gray hair and/or beard (which only means, of course, that your pigmentation cells have dried up), (2) a look of steadfast and thoughtful concentration (probably because you're trying to remember where you left your glasses), (3) a deliberate and dignified manner of entering a room (arthritis), and (4) numerous stories to tell of the challenges you have faced and overcome (some wildly exaggerated, some downright lies).

These being the appearances of wisdom, I'm not surprised that some of the dumbest people I grew up with now have the greatest reputations for being wise.

Wisdom, though, if it's the genuine article, is a good thing to have, though there are times when you'd rather have your hair, your teeth and your short-term memory. (See also **ADVICE, CORRECTIVE CRITICISM, LECTURE, MORALITY, PREACHING.**)

WORD CHOICE.

A very important tool for maintaining the self-esteem of the retiree. In this field, as in most others at the present time, it's not so much what you say, but how you say it that counts, and this will become more and more true as the aging come to make up a larger portion of the population. Soon most of them will be Baby Boomers, and believe me, they won't be called "geezers", "old fogeys" or "old farts", they'll be "mature ladies and gentlemen" and "senior citizens". They won't be "gray-headed", they'll be "distinguished" or "matronly". Their faces won't be "wrinkled", they'll be "rugged". They won't be "not working", they'll be "semi-retired". They won't be "pensioned off", they'll be "drawing an annuity". They'll never be "loafing", they'll be "recharging the batteries". Well, in an age when watered-down education is "inclusive", filthy movies are "edgy", rude celebrities are "candid" and discriminatory legislation is "targeted", why not? (See also **POLITICAL CORRECTNESS.**)

WORK.

The dirtiest of all four-letter words, particularly Mondays just as the alarm goes off. Also "the curse of the drinking classes", to quote Oscar Wilde. Also the curse of the retired, who must work hard at avoiding it. Work is worshipped as a god in North American and European culture, and you must expect a certain amount of social ostracism when you walk away from it for good. Therefore you must be strong, steel yourself, cast off the puritanical addiction to labour and learn the art of relaxing. It will be difficult for awhile, but eventually you will find you can get just as hooked on loafing as you once were to work — and it doesn't have nearly as many unpleasant side effects.

To put this concept into perspective: Whenever the media quotes unemployment statistics, they will say 1.2 million Canadians — or whatever the number is at the time — are looking for work. What they are really looking for, of course, is not so much work as an income, for which they are willing, if necessary, to work. When I first struck out on my own as a young man I wasn't really in love with the idea of picking rocks, pulling up tree roots and chucking them off a cutline (which I did) or piling heavy green lumber at a sawmill in 30-degree weather (which I also did). It was just that I had, in my young life, picked up some of the self-indulgent habits of civilization — things like eating three meals a day, sleeping indoors and wearing clothing. It was to provide those necessities that work was originally pursued. Let's not make it a life-devouring obsession. (For further details on attitudes toward work and how to overcome them see **ENERGY, FREEDOM, GOALS, GUILT, LABOUR, LOAFING, LEISURE, WHEN, WORKAHOLIC, SEMI-RETIREMENT.**)

WORKAHOLIC.

A bright, bouncy, eager, energetic, cheerful, thoroughly tiresome and obnoxious creature. Stay away from him or her whatever you do. Such people are the mortal enemies of retirement, and you don't want to mess with them. When they show up on TV and begin to brag about all the books they have written this year while juggling speaking schedules, exotic hobbies, political and business ventures, switch channels as fast as possible. If it's too late and you find they have tempted you to return to work or bury yourself under a mountain of activities and responsibilities, give me a call. I or one of my friends from Workaholics Anonymous, who have devoted themselves to stamping out the scourge of workaholism, will soon talk you out of such idiocy. But don't call after five o'clock and don't call too often; we're retired, after all.

Let me hasten to add that I bear no ill will towards workaholics. I don't hate them, I only hate their disgusting habit, and in fact pity them. I sincerely hope that some day a cure will be found, perhaps a medication that can be taken orally or by injection. Until then only psychiatric help is available to deal with the deep-seated feelings of inadequacy which they are trying so hard to compensate for with their frenzied activity (I read that, with great satisfaction, somewhere). I try hard to understand this psychological disease — for that is what it is — though I myself have never had even a mild case of it. Some of my acquaintances no doubt refer to me as indolent, when what I really am, obviously, is emotionally well-adjusted. (See also **GUILT, LABOUR, LEISURE, LOAFING, WHEN, WORK.**)

WRINKLES.

Often referred to as Laugh Lines, Marks of Honour, Badges of Courageous Struggle etc. What they really are, of course, is Proof You're Over the Hill. (See also **FACELIFT, PLASTIC SURGERY, SIGNS OF AGING, WORD CHOICE.**)

Y

YARD WORK.

There are two kinds of people: (1) Those who find in yard work great satisfaction, and look forward to having more time for it upon retirement. (2) Those who find in yard work the major reason for their decision to move into a condominium upon retirement. (See also GARDENING.)

YOU'RE OLD WHEN . . .

When you decide that you're long in the tooth, over the hill, fossilized, time-worn, moth-eaten, old as the hills, ripe with age and in your twilight years, then perhaps the time has come when you should stop mixing your metaphors. (See HILL, GOLDEN YEARS, SIGNS OF AGING.)

Z

zzzzzzzzzz.

The sweet sound to be found at the end of a perfect retirement day. Works pretty good in the afternoons too, if you have sense enough not to feel guilty about it. A pleasant thought, in fact, with which to end this book. ZZZZZZZZZZZZZZZZZZZZZZ . . .

CPSIA information can be obtained
at www.ICGtesting.com
Printed in the USA
LVOW04s0702061215
465598LV00013B/38/P